PHalarope Books

PHalarope Books are designed specifically for the amateur naturalist. These volumes represent excellence in natural history publishing. Each book in the PHalarope series is based on a nature course or program at the college or adult education level or is sponsored by a museum or nature center. Each PHalarope Book reflects the author's teaching ability as well as writing ability.

BOOKS IN THE SERIES:

The Curious Naturalist
JOHN MITCHELL and the
Massachusetts Audubon Society.

The Amateur Naturalist's Handbook
VINSON BROWN

The Art of Painting Animals:
A Beginning Artist's Guide to the Portrayal
of Domestic Animals, Wildlife, and Birds
FREDRIC SWENEY

Nature Drawing: A Tool for Learning
CLARE WALKER LESLIE

Outdoor Education: A Manual for Teaching
in Nature's Classroom
MICHAEL LINK, Director, Northwoods Audubon
Center, Minnesota

Nature with Children of All Ages:
Activities and Adventures for Exploring,
Learning, & Enjoying the World Around Us
EDITH A. SISSON, Massachusetts Audubon Society

The Wildlife Observer's Guidebook
CHARLES E. ROTH, Massachusetts Audubon Society

Nature Photography: A Guide to
Better Outdoor Pictures
STAN OSOLINSKI

A Complete Manual of Amateur Astronomy:
Tools and Techniques for
Astronomical Observations
P. CLAY SHERROD with THOMAS L. KOED

365 Starry Nights: An Introduction to
Astronomy for Every Night of the Year
CHET RAYMO

John Mitchell is Editor of *The Curious Naturalist* magazine and assistant editor of publications for the Massachusetts Audubon Society.

THE CURIOUS NATURALIST

ILLUSTRATED BY GORDON MORRISON

JOHN MITCHELL & THE MASSACHUSETTS AUDUBON SOCIETY

A SPECTRUM BOOK

Prentice-Hall, Inc., Englewood Cliffs, New Jersey 07632

Library of Congress Cataloging in Publication Data
Main entry under title:

The Curious naturalist.

(A Spectrum Book)
"Contents of The Curious naturalist originally
appeared in a magazine of the same name published by
the Massachusetts Audubon Society."
Bibliography: p.
1. Natural history. I. Mitchell, John, 1940-
II. Massachusetts Audubon Society
QH45.5.C87 1980   574.974   80-12419
ISBN 0-13-195412-1
ISBN 0-13-195404-0 (pbk.)

The contents of *The Curious Naturalist* originally appeared in a magazine
of the same name, published by the Massachusetts Audubon Society, Lincoln,
Massachusetts 01773.

A SPECTRUM BOOK

Printed in the United States of America
10 9 8 7 6 5 4 3

Lettering on drawings by Leslie Cowperthwaite.
Editorial/production supervision and interior design by Maria Carella.
Page layout by Patricia Palermo.
Cover design by Tony Ferrara Studio, Inc.
Manufacturing buyer: Cathie Lenard.

Prentice-Hall International, Inc., *London*
Prentice-Hall of Australia Pty., Limited, *Sydney*
Prentice-Hall of Canada, Ltd., *Toronto*
Prentice-Hall of India Private, Limited, *New Delhi*
Prentice-Hall of Japan, Inc., *Tokyo*
Prentice-Hall of Southeast Asia Pte., Ltd., *Singapore*
Whitehall Books, Limited, *Wellington, New Zealand*

I would like to thank Mary S. Shakespeare, Chris Graunas, Virginia Jevon, and Leslie Cowperthwaite for their patient attention to certain uninspiring details involved in the production of this book.

INTRODUCTION

There was an old man in our town named Gilly Robinson who more or less served as the unofficial naturalist for the children of the community. Whenever we had a bird with a broken wing or a plant or animal that needed identification, or for that matter, whenever we had a question about natural history in general, we would track up to Gilly's house to get help.

Gilly lived at the edge of a woodland that spread westward to a low ridge. Whenever he wasn't answering questions for children or caring for his collection of orphaned wildlife, he would be off wandering the uninhabited ridges beyond his woodland. According to local legend Gilly used to supplement his income by maintaining a trapline. One day, after a particularly gruesome experience with a trapped fox, he quit his traps and swore he would devote the rest of his life to caring for wildlife.

In retrospect, I realize that Gilly was the mildly eccentric sort of social misfit who nowadays might be living off state aid or institutionalized in some old people's home. But to us, in those days, he was pure hero, a man who fell somewhere between wild Indian, Pan, and a benevolent woods-dwelling Santa Claus. The thing I remember best about Gilly is not his ability to identify plants and animals, but the long Saturday morning rambles we would take with him through the woods behind his "museum." He was in his element in the woods. He seemed energized by the presence of trees and birds and would virtually leap from point to point as he described, in animated detail, the characteristics or uses of some obscure plant. He had an odd habit of holding any interesting object he had found as close to his face as he could, as if he needed to smell the thing, or inspect it in minute detail in order to identify it. This is the image of him I remember best, a skinny goatlike man hopping from tree trunk to tree trunk, pointing out a variety of local natural wonders to his accompanying tribe of children.

I don't know for sure, but I would guess that Gilly is dead now, and I mean that both literally and figuratively. He was old even when we knew him, and even though energetic nature types such as Gilly have a way of outliving mere mortals, I would say that he is no longer living alone at the edge of his beloved woodland. What I am more certain about, and more disturbed about, is the figurative death of Gilly. His type has been institutionalized now, or rather he has become an institution.

Except perhaps in some isolated rural areas, there are very few of the semieccentric men and women left who served as the resident natural history guides for the children of a community. It is still possible to get the type of information that Gilly provided, but you have to dig to do it. Gilly not only identified things for us, he would always build elaborate stories to help us remember whatever it was he was describing. Some of these stories were pure folklore. For example, I will always think of the butternut tree as the witches' tree because Gilly told us that once a year the witches would come out and wander through the night woods ironing flat all the rough bark of the butternut trees. That may not be a scientifically accurate reason for the flattened, ironed appearance of butternut bark, but

I have had no trouble identifying the tree in any season ever since.

The point is that Gilly's figurative death has left a void. Nowadays, in order to identify a plant or animal you have to go to the school science department, or to the library, or if there happens to be one nearby, to the local nature center. The people who you consult at any of these various institutions may or may not be able to answer your question outright, but it is doubtful whether they would be able to answer with the same richness or flare that Gilly did. And certainly the milieu will not be the same. Gilly always worked at home, in the woods, or from his hand-hewn bench on the south side of his house.

What is more likely is that the official at the school or nature center will have to consult a book to answer your question. And that leads to another problem. It is very easy to find a book that will help you to identify accurately any plant or animal you may have found—there are scores of field guides presently in print on nearly every natural history subject, and new ones, embodying newer and simpler techniques, are published annually. But it is harder to find out why the damsel fly is sometimes called the snake doctor, or why the bark of the butternut tree is flattened. Such information was the province of the old school of nature guides such as Gilly.

Not that such books didn't exist. At the turn of the century natural history books that offered little tidbits of interesting fact and folklore about common plants and animals were abundant. But unfortunately, most of these books are now out of print. The fact is, in spite of a re-surgence of interest in natural history and the environment, there is a small empty nook in the body of the subject that was once the place of the less scientific but in some ways more humane side of the natural world.

The Curious Naturalist is a modest at-tempt to fill that empty nook. It is a book that is intended to get you out of the houses and the libraries and the class-rooms and into the woods and the fields. It is by no means an attempt to identify all the plants and animals that you will find there—the new field guides can do that. Nor is the book an attempt to offer the type of information that was provided by the old school of natural history leaders such as Gilly. That is something I believe cannot be done in print. The purpose of *The Curious Naturalist* is to give you a sense of the complexities and richness of the outdoors—the spirit of the woods and fields that the older teachers like Gilly used to impart to their students. More than anything else, the book is intended to pique your curiosity so that you will get the urge to explore further the mysteries that are at work in any natural habitat. Later you can consult the books and the libraries and the school science depart-ments.

If there is a guiding principle in *The Curi-ous Naturalist,* it is the concept of the field trip. That is not to say that the book is a step-by-step guide through all the var-ious habitats in the four seasons, but it is intended to convey the feeling that any good naturalist will give on such a trip. On any given field trip, through any habi-tat, in any season, there are certain orders of living things that you are bound to en-counter. These include any number of species of insects, birds, mammals and reptiles and amphibians, as well as in-numerable species of herbaceous plants and trees that provide food and shelter for these animals. The problem is that any attempt to categorically list and identify this vast panoply of life can only serve to induce a state of boredom in the erstwhile student of natural history. On the other hand, it is hoped that a little morsel of information about a particular plant or animal, or a little fact or piece of folklore about a certain species of tree, will create a desire to learn more. Any sharp nature leader knows this. A good field trip is a disorderly accumulation of facts, figures, identifying characteristics, and the like. But when all this information is put together, the sense of wholeness that is such a critical part of ecological understanding should be strikingly clear.

With this in mind, we have scattered through the pages of *The Curious Naturalist* odd bits of information on the living things that you might encounter on a field trip through some local habitat. The basic organization of the book is sea-sonal; each of the four sections deals with the subjects that you would find of interest during any given season. Of course the natural world is a constantly changing scenario, so obviously you will find more about certain species of plants and animals in one section than you will in another. Birds such as warblers, for example, are much more common in spring than they are in midsummer or winter. Mammal tracks that appear com-monly in the winter landscape are dif-ficult to find in the dry grasses of sum-mer.

By contrast, you will find that some plants and animals are treated in certain seasons specifically because of their absence. For example, where are all the bees and wasps in winter? What happens to the chipmunks that fill the summer woods? Gilly Robinson always used to make a point of describing the richness of the summer woods in the midst of the barren fields of winter. To emphasize his point he would show us the empty, wind-torn birds' nests and the ripped webs of the fall webworms.

The field trip is not the only guiding principle for The Curious Naturalist. The book is actually a compilation of pages from various issues of a magazine published by the Massachusetts Audubon Society. In the early 1960s staff members of Massachusetts Audubon founded a small four-page publication called The Curious Naturalist that was intended to help beginning naturalists get a better grasp of the subject. The original concept of the publication was to treat a single subject in each issue, including as much related material as seemed pertinent. One issue would be devoted to habitat, for example, or to predators. The concept works very well in a field such as natural history where everything is interrelated anyway, and over the years the publication grew into a small magazine. The number of pages increased, a second color was added, and readership extended far beyond the borders of Massachusetts. Unfortunately, the budget for the publication did not grow accordingly, and in later years The Curious Naturalist found itself constantly in the red. What is more, the magazine was now in competition with a number of four-color children's magazines with substantially larger budgets and promotion departments. In spite of the integrity of the magazine, subscriptions leveled off and it looked like the publication was going to go out of print.

The magazine had already experienced a number of drastic changes in format in its fifteen-year history, and rather than drop it altogether the staff decided to take the magazine through one more change. Several of us spent that summer kicking around new ideas. What we had in mind was some kind of small quarterly magazine that would have everything in it—fiction, games, natural history articles, a lot of artwork and photos, a few how-to columns on gardening, farming, and so on—and all that on a severely limited budget. The overall concept was to get back to the intent of the original Curious Naturalist. In recent years the magazine had been reaching for a more sophisticated audience and found itself dealing with such hefty and unwieldy subjects as worldwide energy production and extinction. We wanted to give some good old-fashioned, homegrown information to our readers.

Once we had a format established we called in a group of technical consultants. Children from local schools brought their lunch over one day, and we had a heavy confrontation on the front lawn of the Massachusetts Audubon editorial offices. Along with lunch, the kids brought their notorious gift for honesty. We presented our ideas to them, and they unerringly shot down every one of them. It turns out they wanted everything we couldn't afford to give them; that is, full color, posters, a magazine that came every week, and so on.

We were already having our suspicions before the meeting because of financial considerations, and so we scrapped a few of the ideas. Then after a few days we scrapped a little more, and then finally we scrapped the whole idea of a magazine as such. What we decided to do was to put together a quarterly publication that simply gave its readers—no matter what age—some basic information on natural history. No overriding educational concept, no lesson plans, simply facts—the type of things that beginning naturalists or anyone interested in the subject in any way might want to know. The idea had one strong argument in its favor. If after four or eight issues the magazine failed, we could always put the pages together and sell it as a book.

The magazine went to press in early September and hit the delivery date right on target—the autumnal equinox. A week or so later the first responses began to come in. Except for one obscure complaint about picturing mushrooms, they were all favorable. In fact as the month progressed, it appeared that in a small way we were experiencing the phenomenon of rave reviews, something we had not expected; after all, we were simply telling facts. One nature educator wrote to say he felt it was the best nature magazine in print. The Curious Naturalist is, in fact, still in print, and is a modest success story, although we still can't afford a promotion department.

The format that got the rave reviews is simplicity itself. Each page is a treatment of some common phenomenon in the natural world, be it plant, animal, or some physical object. Half of the treatment is visual, to give some idea of what the thing looks like, and half is text, to give you a few facts about whatever is being treated. Like the year, the book is divided into four sections, and like the seasons themselves each section begins where all seasons begin—in the night sky. The first page of each section is a treatment of the more common constellations that you will see overhead in the northern hemisphere in the corresponding season. The following page shows in closer detail the constellation or star that would be most obvious at that time of year. Rough and hand-drawn as they may appear, the sky charts work. I couldn't remember the name of a certain constellation one night and couldn't find my star guide, so I used the pages of The Curious Naturalist and found what I was looking for. Nevertheless, as with all these pages, I don't recommend that you rely on them for identification. They are simply takeoff points to help you understand what is out there. In connection with this, you will find at the bottom of each page one or two recommendations for further reading. The books should help you identify or learn more about the subject treated on the page.

You will find that the subjects following the first two pages on the sky are grouped more or less according to families or orders—three or four pages on birds, for example, or five or six pages dealing with plants. As I have said, there is more about certain families or orders in certain seasons; but in the end everything should fall together so that you get at least some sense of the complexities of living things that are at work in any natural environment throughout the year.

The habitats treated in the book are the

ones that are accessible. High mountains, deserts, tundra, jungles, and even the sea and its shores are skipped over. Except for the coast, unless you have access to some miraculous transportation system, or live in a remote area, these are not the habitats that you will find just beyond your backyard or just beyond your average city limits. The aim is to get you out into the nearest wild place, whether that is a vacant city lot grown over with weeds or a wooded ridge beyond the highest meadow on your family farm.

Unfortunately, one of the tragedies of modern life is that the nearest vacant lot or nearest woodland is often a half-hour drive from the place where you live. For this reason I have included information on a number of species of plants and animals that are commonly found in the suburban backyard. This is not as much of a copout as it may seem. Recent statistics suggest that a large percentage of the American population now lives in suburbia, and wildlife biologists are now studying the role of the backyard in the life cycles of certain species of insects, birds, and mammals. Most of the land around the populated centers of the United States is now developed in one way or another, and the manner in which these miniature land holdings are managed for wildlife can make or break the existence of certain native species. A minor example will serve to illustrate. In recent decades starlings and house sparrows have evicted the native bluebird from its natural nesting cavities. Enough properly placed bluebird houses in the backyards of suburbia and exurbia could insure the success of this threatened species. Moths offer another example. Commercially sold black lights are intended to attract

and kill mosquitoes, but the lights also attract and kill a number of species of rare and periodic moths that entomologists spend years searching for. The point is, what you do or do not do in your backyard can affect local wildlife populations. A man's house may be his castle, but his backyard belongs to the planet.

With this in mind, you will find in each seasonal section a page or two entitled "Backyard Sanctuary." These pages will offer some ideas for things you can do around your yard either to attract wildlife or to help certain rare or threatened species such as the bluebird. Some of these projects involve a certain amount of planting or construction, but generally, turning your property into a miniature wildlife sanctuary is not at all difficult. In fact, in some ways the best thing you can do is nothing, that is, you can simply allow your yard to grow up naturally. Like a field, the backyard is essentially a disturbed area, and like any such environment, the natural tendency of the area is to return to its original state, which in most sections of the country, would be forestland. Land in the early stages of the return, the environment the ecologists refer to as the old-field or seral state, is one of the most beneficial for wildlife.

I can personally attest to the efficiency of such an environment. A few years ago my family and I moved into an old farmhouse. The land around the house, which was once intensively cultivated, had been let go, and was in the process of returning to forest. Wildlife abounded in the area. In fact, there was almost too much wildlife. Nightly we were plagued with skunks under the house, foxes in the chicken coop, raccoons, and similar visitations.

That is not to say you have to let your land run wild in order to study local wildlife populations. Even a carefully manicured lawn attracts a certain number of species of native plants and animals. Daily any number of small adventures and cycles are played out in the backyards of suburbia, most of them unnoticed by the average house dweller. Some of the techniques and equipment used to observe these cycles are illustrated in the book. For example, try sweeping the longer grasses of some unmanicured section of your yard with a homemade insect net. You'll be surprised at the number of different species you come up with. Actually even a well-clipped lawn has its share of wildlife. A recent study found that there are just as many individual insects on a cropped lawn as in uncut grasses, although the species are different in the two habitats.

Even the simple addition of a bird feeder or wildlife feeding station can make a difference in the number of animals around the yard. Feeders attract a large number of birds, and they have a way of attracting mammals as well, even mammals such as raccoons that aren't necessarily feeding there. Watch your feeder at night for the silent drift of visiting flying squirrels. If you live anywhere near a woodland, chances are these secretive, nocturnal squirrels have been visiting your feeder regularly. Ground-dwelling mammals such as meadow voles and rabbits and even skunks and possums tend to visit the feeder as well. The fact is, for all its civilized, manicured ambiance, the backyard is a natural stage upon which primal rituals are played.

The Curious Naturalist is a book intended to get you out into the woods and fields exploring natural environments; but I will admit that there are such things as rainy days. Although I personally enjoy the woods in foul weather, I have included a number of nature-related crafts in the book to help while away stormy days and nights.

There is sound precedent in this, I believe. Crafts more or less go hand in hand with close observation and can be a valuable tool in learning about the natural world. In fact, a rising number of outdoor educators subscribe to the philosophy that anything that will get you in close contact with nature, from casual field study to cross-country skiing or crafts can offer a valuable introduction to more intense study. One of the things I remember about Gilly Robinson is that he was forever picking up little bits of natural material or sawing off burls or interestingly shaped branches. He would transport these various discoveries back to his house and transform them into decorations or furniture for what he used to refer to as his nature museum. The place was indeed a wonder of creativity. His dining room table consisted of three great slabs of oak set on legs cut from branches. The corners and walls of his main room were decorated with birds' nests, mounted owls, and dried plants, and scattered around the room were any number of nature crafts in various stages of development. Gilly was a master of the artists' fungus. Each year, he would collect as many of the mushrooms as he could find and then spend the winter painting or etching landscapes on the white undersides.

I am not suggesting that you turn your house into a museum, but there are a number of crafts that can fill the empty spaces of the long winter nights, and help you learn something about natural history at the same time. You will notice that most of the crafts mentioned on these pages relate directly to some subject that has been discussed earlier. For example, in the summer chapter there is a treatment of common rushes and reeds. Later on in the same section you will find a page that tells you how to make a rush mat. Some of the craft ideas included, such as snowshoes or the snow snake, are not only constructed from things that are collected in the woods and fields, they are intended to get you back outdoors once they are completed.

Finally, to keep you in tune with the seasonal cycles, which are such an important part of any natural environment, on the last page of each section there is a week-by-week calendar of natural events. By necessity, this calendar is general. Bird arrivals, the first song of the peepers in spring, and the flowering of trees and herbaceous plants are entirely local events. A calendar such as this can hardly serve to pinpoint when this or that event will take place in the area in which you live. If you want an accurate record of the natural events that occur in your area, you can use *The Curious Naturalist* calendar as a model and prepare your own. Better yet, keep a running notebook of the seasons. Such records can be valuable tools for understanding natural cycles. In any case, the purpose of the calendar in the back of each section of

The Curious Naturalist, as of the whole book, is to sharpen your awareness of the natural changes that are taking place around you.

Even though one of the guiding principles of this book is the concept of the field trip, *The Curious Naturalist* is not necessarily intended to be used in the fields. It is better studied before you go out for a walk, or after you come back. The subject matter treated is of such an elementary and common nature that on any given walk you will quite possibly encounter some of the things that are mentioned. For example, in some areas it is difficult to take a nature walk in late summer and *not* see the webs of the fall webworm. In all likelihood you have been seeing them all along. Similarly, it would be hard to cross a pasture in midsummer without scaring up at least one Carolina grasshopper. Both of these insects are treated in the summer section of the book.

This is not intended to be a book for advanced naturalists. It is designed for the beginner, for the person who knows little or nothing about natural history, although in these days of overspecialization it is possible that the advanced student of herpetology or botany might be able to find something interesting as well. But the very simplicity of the approach creates a problem: Where do you go for more information? In addition to the books listed at the bottom of each page you will find an extensive bibliography in the back. Some of the books listed are older and may be difficult to find, but in some ways that may be a sign that they are good. As I pointed out earlier, some of the most informative books in the field of natural history seem to be out of print.

In connection with the bibliography you will find information on source material that is available through the Massachusetts Audubon Society. Over the years the various departments of the society have published a variety of material covering a number of natural history subjects. This includes among other things pamphlets on such practical matters as what to do about bats in your attic, the life cycles of stinging insects, and the like.

We also included in this list information on how to order back issues of the old *Curious Naturalist* magazine. Some of the back issues of the original magazine are perennial favorites with teachers and parents, such as the issue on biomes. I have also included in this section a subscription blank for the new *Curious Naturalist*. If you like what you see in this book, for four dollars you can have more of the same, four times a year.

In an odd sort of way, if used diligently, *The Curious Naturalist* could serve as a short introductory course to the general field of natural science. If you carefully use the book through the various seasons, following up on all the recommended reading, working out some of the backyard sanctuary projects, and perhaps making some of the crafts, you might end up with a fairly solid background in field natural history. That is not to say you would know the etiology of the migration of the monarch butterfly, or have a working knowledge of the complex field of taxonomy. But you might have some of the basic type of interesting information that Gilly Robinson always seemed to have at his fingertips. And if you do your homework properly, that is, if you spend as much time as possible in the woods and fields, you may well get your knowledge from running brooks and trees, rather than from books.

Spring

Some clear night in early February, step outside and get yourself to a place where you can get a good view of the eastern sky. If you watch carefully, sometime between seven and nine o'clock you may notice, just over the horizon, a large curved formation of stars that looks a little like a backward question mark or a sickle. This is the constellation Leo, the Lion, and it is the first sign of spring. Nearly two months later, on the twenty-first of March, the sun will cross an imaginary line in the sky known as the ecliptic. On that day, the day and the night will be equal in length, and spring will officially begin.

It may seem odd to look into the night sky to mark the beginning of events that will take place on earth, but natural occurrences such as the arrival of spring are notoriously unpredictable, and through-out history the great wheel of the night sky has provided man with an unerring chart to help him track the seasons.

In keeping with the unpredictable nature of the changing seasons, here on earth there may be a few snowstorms after the twenty-first of March, and there will be times when it seems that the warmth of spring will never materialize. But with the rising of the Lion in the eastern sky, there can be no turning back: the switches have been thrown on the great engine of the seasons, and everywhere in the woods and fields the small often un-noticed natural events that make up the early part of the season are beginning to fire off. By late February the sap is rising in the trees, the skunk cabbage is poking up through the moist soils of the swamps, and in the woodlands the cardinals and chickadees are singing their spring songs.

Slowly the well-recognized events of spring begin to occur: the pussy willows fluff out; the crocus, the snow drops, and the other garden flowers bloom; and then some night late in March or early April there will be a heavy rain—the air will warm and the voice of the frogs will be heard once more.

There is perhaps no other event in the natural world that is as characteristic of a season as a full chorus of spring peepers. It is not only that the voices of living things are calling once more after the long silence of winter, there is something about the atmosphere in which the chorus takes place that epitomizes the season. There is a certain moist smell in the air on rainy spring nights, slow mists rise from rafts of ice floating in dark marshes, everywhere on roads through wet areas the small white forms of migrating spring peepers, wood frogs, green frogs, and pickerel frogs appear, and all around you the air will be filled with a high bell-like ringing, a little like a distant horse-drawn sleigh. That distant chorus is the voice of the spring peeper, a small tree frog no larger than the end of a little finger. Throughout history naturalists have referred to it as the voice of spring.

In actuality you may be a long way from the pond or marsh that the peepers are calling from. The voice of spring peepers can carry as much as a mile on still spring nights, and once you learn to recognize the song there will be nights when it is difficult to escape their incessant calling. The sound will accompany you through spring, a sort of background music to the events that will be taking place around you during the season.

Even before the night chorus of the spring peepers begins, amphibian life will be stirring in the woods and ponds—early spring is the season of amphibians. As early as the first of March, sometimes while snows are still lingering in the deep woods, Jefferson's red-backed, and spotted salamanders, will stir from their winter hibernating places beneath rocks and logs and begin to move towards temporary ponds, where they will mate and lay eggs.

More obvious perhaps to the beginning naturalist is the chorus of the wood frogs. If you take a walk in the woods shortly after the ice melts out from the ponds, you may hear the dull ducklike call of these masked frogs. Creep silently up to the shallow pond from which they are calling and you may see one or two of them, legs outspread, floating in a ripple in the clear water. Approach too quickly and the chorus will fall silent—wood frogs are suspicious of intrusion. Don't look for wood frogs in deeper pools or permanent ponds; they are creatures of the shallow temporary ponds that collect in damp wooded areas and treed swamps in the spring. The eggs will hatch, tadpoles will develop, and the frogs will leave the pond early in the summer before the shallow waters dry up.

Even if you don't happen to hear the chorus of the wood frogs, a walk in the woods at this time of year can be an exhilarating and sometimes enlightening experience. The snow has gone, and for the first time since fall you can stride smoothly over the earth. It is no longer necessary to pick and trudge your way through the deep snows. Not only that, there is a quality of light in the early spring woods that occurs at no other time of year. November has a vaguely similar light, a sort of dry, dusty brown; but the light of the March woods has a moist clear texture that seems to enrich the colors of landscape. Tree bark and rocks seem to have a damp glow of their own.

Had they the consciousness to perceive it, no other form of life would be more conscious of the light of the early spring woods than the various species of wild flowers that bloom there. It is the length and in some ways the quality of the light that causes them to bloom. The short period between the onset of warm weather sometime in April and the leafing out of the trees sometime in early May is the only time that the sun can reach the woodland floor, and some of the most delicate and beautiful wildflowers take advantage of this brief period to bloom. During late April, in the proper area, the woodlands will be alive with bloodroot, violets, trout lilly, and Dutchman's-breeches. The show creates one of the many spectacles of nature that occur throughout the year, everywhere the delicate, ephemeral wild flowers are blossoming out. The dull, energetic chorus of the wood frogs will be throbbing somewhere in the distance, and the brief, eerie calls of the phoebe and other early bird migrants will pierce the long silence that held sway through the winter.

But all that is a temporary interlude. The brief season of early spring is about to come to an end. In some ways it could be said that there are eight seasons, rather than four. Early spring is as different from late spring as summer is from winter. Similarly, early summer and late summer, once you learn to recognize the sub-tleties, are two different seasons, each with its own events and wildlife activities.

No one is more aware of these differences than the alert naturalist; and there are a number of traditional rituals that naturalists observe throughout the season in order to stay in touch. One of these is a walk in the rain along some back road in a swampy area in order to view the night migration of the amphibians. Another is a walk in the late April woods to witness the blooming of the wild flowers. But perhaps the most cherished of these various rituals is a visit to some nearby woodcock dancing ground. Woodcocks, small, squat birds with long bills, will have been in the north for a number of weeks. But it is not until early April that the actual flights begin.

Partly perhaps because of its secretiveness, the event is reminiscent of some obscure, seldom-seen ritual among an undiscovered primitive tribe. Throughout the year, woodcocks inhabit secluded woodland areas, where they probe the moist soils for earthworms and other invertebrates. It is only now, in April, that they emerge from oblivion, and even then it is only to the initiated that they reveal themselves.

In spite of this, the event is not hard to observe. All you have to do is go to a clearing at dusk near a wooded area where woodcocks are likely to feed. The first indication that you have found the proper place will be a short "peent" that is repeated again and again like a high-toned duck quack. Follow the "peent" to the clearing and you will be rewarded with a flight display that rivals any military air show for tricks. For eleven months of the year the woodcock spends its life facing downward towards the dank soil where it feeds. Now it suddenly takes to the sky, as if it had to make up for its time spent in mud.

After a few minutes of circling and bowing as it repeats its call, the woodcock takes to the air. It will climb higher and higher above the trees against the darkening sky until it may be lost to view. Then, in splendor, it will drop. The descending flight is punctuated with barrel rolls, loop-the-loops, side flights, twists, and similar aerial acrobatics, and all the while, the wind wails through specialized primary feathers so that the flight is accompanied by a series of soft warbles and whistles. It is only after this elaborate display that the woodcock lands, usually only a few feet from its original takeoff point, to begin the whole process over again.

There is one other ritual that devoted naturalists attend to before spring officially comes to an end, and that is an early morning walk to observe the warbler migration. Although, like the woodcock flights, the passage of the warblers is often unnoticed by the uninitiated, the migration takes place in the backyards of suburbia and in easily accessible places, such as nearby parks and woodlands.

The wave of warbler migration begins to crest about a month after the woodcock flights begin and will continue on into late May. By all accounts, it is one of the great events of natural history, involving millions of individuals. What is more, it is easy and altogether pleasant to observe. Some morning in May(the second week in

the month is the traditional viewing date), get up early, and take a pair of binoculars to the nearest wooded area. As the sun warms the trees, and the insects become more active, the forest canopy will become alive with the quick forms of darting birds. Warblers are sometimes difficult to identify, but you don't have to be an experienced bird watcher to enjoy the spectacle; the numbers alone should serve to impress you. Everywhere, from the highest upper branches to the forest floor, the woods will be alive with these small, brightly colored insect-eating birds. Some fly out to snap up some unseen insect. Some, like the black-and-white warbler, circle the trunks of trees tirelessly, while others, like the oven bird or the Louisiana waterthrush, shuffle amidst the leaf litter on the forest floor.

The passage of the warblers marks the end of what might be termed the first season. Slowly, during the second week in May, tree leaves will blossom out. Then a few days later the full leaf will appear. Abruptly, in the space of a week or so, the sharp, brindled light that has characterized the woods since late October will disappear and the forest floor will be obscured in rich shadows. The threat of snow and ice is finally banished and in a prelude to summer, the second season begins.

Slowly, as the warm weather progresses, the traditional spring of the layman makes itself obvious. The leaves are out on the trees, flowers in gardens and fields begin to bloom, the lilacs blossom, the air has that rich warm scent of life, and everywhere birds are calling. Most striking of all, perhaps, is the air. Early spring, even warm days in April, may have something of a damp nip. But once the tree leaves are out, the easy warmth of summer is felt. The season now seems closer to summer than to spring and slowly, as the warm nights seep in, the great constellation the Lion rises later and later and slowly creeps westward across the sky. By late June it will give way to other, more spectacular constellations that will mark the arrival of summer.

The Spring Sky

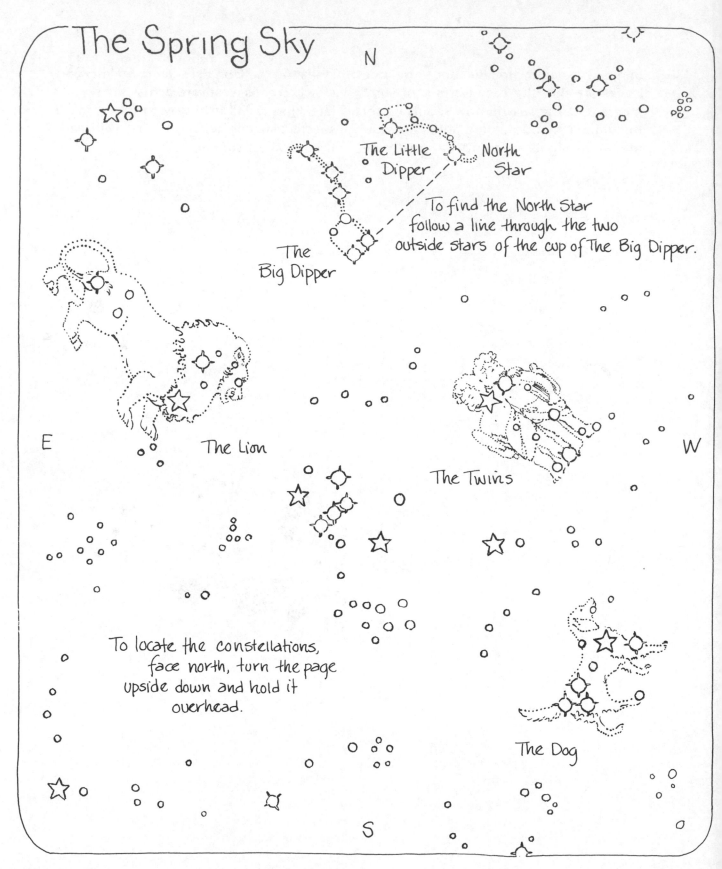

N

The Little Dipper

North Star

To find the North Star follow a line through the two outside stars of the cup of The Big Dipper.

The Big Dipper

The Lion

E

The Twins

W

To locate the constellations, face north, turn the page upside down and hold it overhead.

The Dog

S

For Further Information: <u>Find the Constellations</u>, H. A. Rey, Houghton Mifflin Company,

The Lion

The Big Dipper

The appearance of the constellation The Lion in the southeastern sky in late March is one of the first signs of spring. The stars that form The Lion's head and neck look like the curving blade of a sickle.

N

You can locate the sickle-shaped head of The Lion by following an imaginary line made by the two back stars of the bowl of The Big Dipper.

The Lion

Face south — and hold the page over your head. The Lion will appear on your left side at about 8 o'clock at night.

For Further Information: <u>The Stars</u>, H.A. Rey, Houghton Mifflin.

WHERE TO PUT A BIRDHOUSE

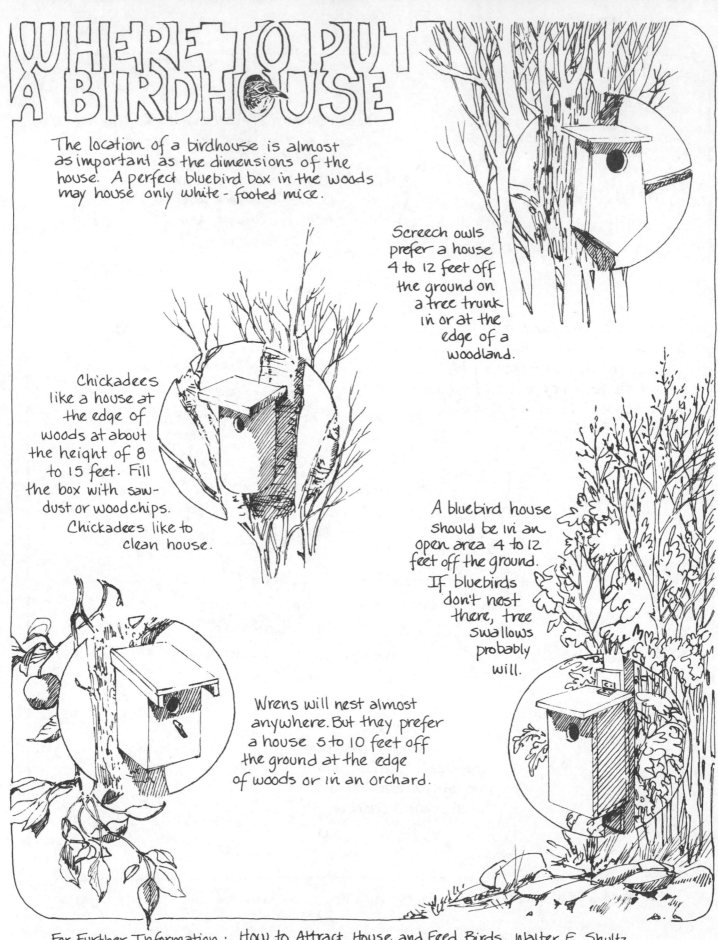

The location of a birdhouse is almost as important as the dimensions of the house. A perfect bluebird box in the woods may house only white-footed mice.

Screech owls prefer a house 4 to 12 feet off the ground on a tree trunk in or at the edge of a woodland.

Chickadees like a house at the edge of woods at about the height of 8 to 15 feet. Fill the box with sawdust or woodchips. Chickadees like to clean house.

A bluebird house should be in an open area 4 to 12 feet off the ground. If bluebirds don't nest there, tree swallows probably will.

Wrens will nest almost anywhere. But they prefer a house 5 to 10 feet off the ground at the edge of woods or in an orchard.

For Further Information: How to Attract, House and Feed Birds, Walter E. Shultz, Collier Macmillan.

SPRING BIRD ARRIVALS

APRIL

1	2	3	4
Tree Swallow	Phoebe	House Wren	Catbird
Dark green back, white underneath.	Brownish back, flicks tail.	Tiny, with brown back and a curved bill.	Grey with black cap.

MAY

1	2	3	4
Northern Oriole	Scarlet Tanager	Indigo Bunting	Wood Pewee
Brilliant orange, high in treetops.	Bright red, black wings.	Bright blue, sings from exposed perch.	Whistles word "Pewee".

For Further Information: How to Know the Birds, Roger Tory Peterson, New American Library.

BIRDS AROUND A POND

For sheer variety, a pond in spring is one of the best places to find birds. Early morning and late evening are the best times to visit the pond.

Belted Kingfisher

Tree swallows visit ponds to hunt for insects.

The mallard is perhaps the most common duck in populated areas. Look for the green head of the male. A typical inhabitant of park ponds.

The green heron sometimes withdraws the typical long neck and takes on the appearance of a brown crow.

Spotted sandpipers run along the muddy shores of ponds. Watch for the peculiar bobbing motion.

For Further Information: <u>Birds of North America</u>, Robbins, Golden Press.

WARBLER WAVE

Even if you can't identify the birds, an early morning walk on the second weekend in May is an experience. It is then that the wave of bird migration crests. Shrubs and tree-tops will be crowded with the darting forms of passing warblers.

The chestnut-sided warbler is more commonly heard than seen. Its call, "Please, Please, Pleased to Meetcha," is one of the common songs of the spring morning.

Chestnut-sided Warbler

Prairie Warbler

Black-and-white Warbler

Yellow Warbler

Yellow-rumped Warbler

Yellowthroat

Watch for the yellow warbler in suburban shrubby areas and the edges of wetlands.

Unlike most warblers, the yellow-rumped will feed on berries. They prefer insects, however, and can be seen darting in the tree-tops during migration. Watch for the yellow rump.

The small zebra-like bird circling tree trunks in late April is the black-and-white warbler.

Watch for the black mask of the yellow-throat. Common in wet areas.

The song of the prairie warbler sounds a little like a spinning coin. A common sound in woodlands in May.

For Further Information: <u>A Field Guide to the Birds</u>, Roger Tory Peterson, Houghton Mifflin.

WOODCOCK WATCHING

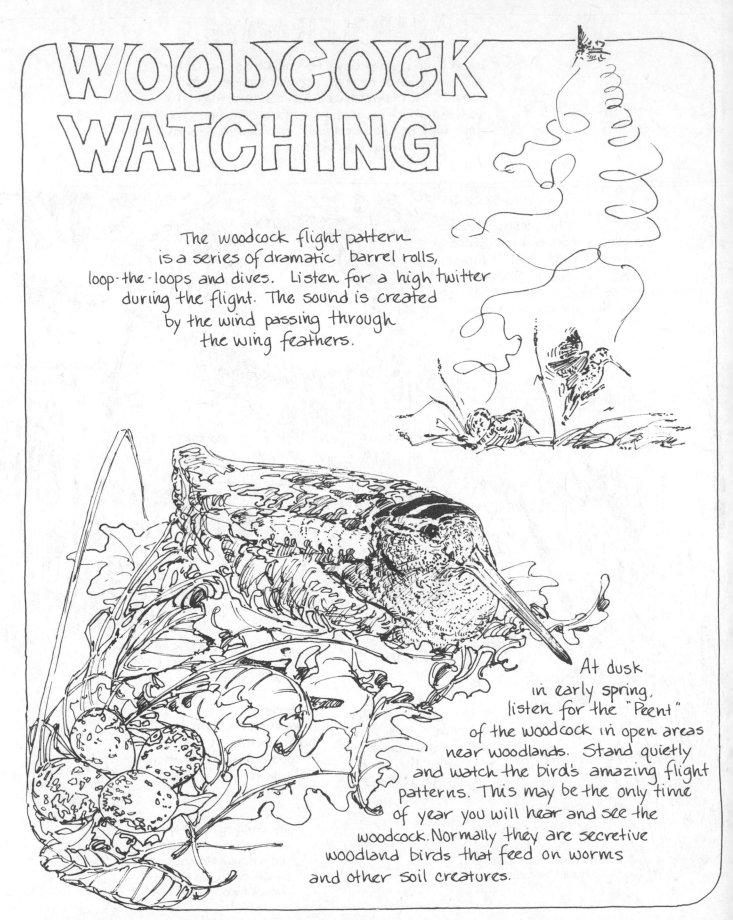

The woodcock flight pattern is a series of dramatic barrel rolls, loop-the-loops and dives. Listen for a high twitter during the flight. The sound is created by the wind passing through the wing feathers.

At dusk in early spring, listen for the "Peent" of the woodcock in open areas near woodlands. Stand quietly and watch the bird's amazing flight patterns. This may be the only time of year you will hear and see the woodcock. Normally they are secretive woodland birds that feed on worms and other soil creatures.

For Further Information: The Life of Birds Noel Carl Welty, Alfred A. Knopf.

WOODPECKER SIGNS

The loud hammering of woodpeckers is one of the most typical sounds of the spring morning.

Downy Woodpecker: A small version of the hairy woodpecker. Males of both downy and hairy have a red patch on the back of the head.

Hairy Woodpecker: Slightly smaller than a robin, boldly marked with black and white.

Woodpeckers do not eat wood. They hammer holes in trees to get at insects which feed under the bark. Woodpeckers play an important role in maintaining the general health of a forest.

Pileated Woodpecker: A large crow-sized woodpecker. They are not as common as the other woodpeckers on this page. Flies with a bold rolling pattern. Makes large rectangular holes.

Flicker: A yellow-brown woodpecker with a curved bill. Flickers often feed on ants.

Look up: Large chunks of wood at the base of a tree may be a sign of a pileated woodpecker.

Yellow-bellied Sapsucker: Look for neat rows of holes in trees. Sapsuckers feed on sap that drips from holes that they drill.

For Further Information: <u>A Field Guide to the Birds</u>, Roger Tory Peterson, Houghton Mifflin.

AMPHIBIANS
of the SPRING
NIGHT

Take a flashlight to some deserted road near a pond or wetland on the first rainy spring night, and see if you can find some of the frogs and salamanders identified on these pages. Look for them crossing the road and in the shallow ponds. Amphibians require moist conditions. That is why they prefer rainy nights for their migrations.

Spotted Salamander: Watch for the glistening black back and the rich yellow spots. Formerly one of the most common salamanders. Now threatened by acid rains.

Red Eft: Orange color, yellow spots.

Blue-spotted Salamander: Looks like old-fashioned enamel ware.

Red-backed Salamander: Found under logs and rocks.

Jefferson Salamander: Difficult to tell apart from the blue-spotted.

Bluish tint to skin.

SALAMANDERS

Certain species of salamanders are now threatened because of acid rains and snows which are created by air pollutants. Acidic pond water prevents development of the salamander embryo.

For Further Information: <u>A Field Guide to Reptiles & Amphibians of Eastern and Central North America</u>, Roger Conant, Houghton Mifflin.

FROGS Frog Calls

The best way to locate an active amphibian breeding pond is by the loud jingle-bell-like call of spring peepers.

Spring Peeper
Call: High bell-like whistle. Spring peepers have dark brown X's on their backs.

Green Frog
Call: Dull twang like a tuned-down banjo. Green frogs have yellowish throats. Their eardrums are about equal to the size of their eyes.

American Toad Call: A long trill. Toads do not cause warts. They do have warts on their backs. That may account for the legend.

Pickerel Frog Call: A short snore. Back marked with obvious squares.

Wood Frog
Call: Duck-like quack. Wood frogs are usually the first to call in spring. Wood frogs have a black mask, like a bandit.

For Further Information: <u>The Frog Book</u>; Mary C. Dickerson, Dover Publications. <u>Spring Peepers</u>, Judy Hawes, Let's-Read-and-Find-Out Science Book, Thomas Crowell.

IDENTIFICATION
of AMPHIBIAN EGGS

	WHERE FOUND	DESCRIPTION
Toad	under water in quiet pools	long spirals with eggs encased in jelly
Wood Frog	under water attached to plants	individual spheres in a mass 4 inches across
Spring Peeper	under water attached to plants	single eggs
Blue-spotted Salamander	on vegetation or sticks under water	strung out in clumps
Spotted Salamander	on sticks under water or free near surface	round globs, sometimes turn green

For Further Information: <u>Reptiles & Amphibians</u>, Herbert S. Zim & Hobart M. Smith, Golden Press.

HATCH A TOAD

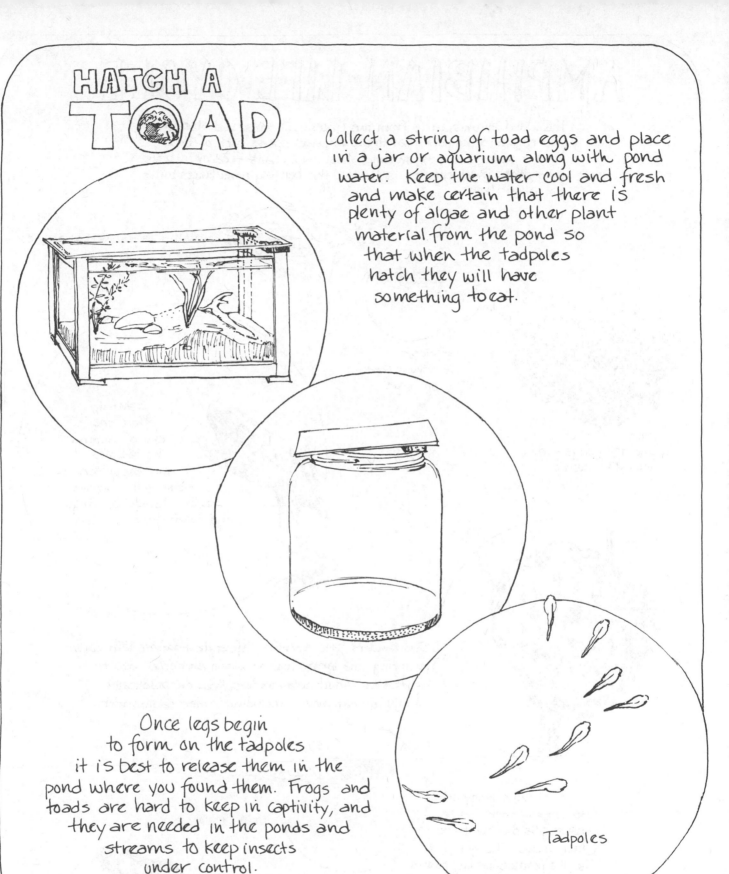

Collect a string of toad eggs and place in a jar or aquarium along with pond water. Keep the water cool and fresh and make certain that there is plenty of algae and other plant material from the pond so that when the tadpoles hatch they will have something to eat.

Once legs begin to form on the tadpoles it is best to release them in the pond where you found them. Frogs and toads are hard to keep in captivity, and they are needed in the ponds and streams to keep insects under control.

Tadpoles

For Further Information: <u>What I Like About Toads</u>, Judy Hawes, Let's-Read-and-Find-Out-Science Book, Thomas Crowell Co.

AMPHIBIAN LIFE CYCLE

The word amphibian is from the Greek. It means double life and refers to the fact that these animals spend part of their lives in water, and part on land. Most amphibians feed on insects and other invertebrates, although the bullfrog sometimes will eat other frogs.

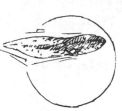

Within a few weeks tadpoles will begin to develop legs.

Tadpoles, or larvae, feed on algae.

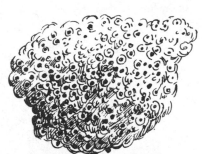

Frog and toad eggs form jelly-like clumps.

Generally, before the end of summer the tadpoles leave the water, some still carrying tails. As adults, frogs and toads feed on insects.

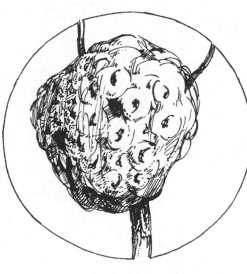

Salamanders have a similar lifestyle. Eggs are laid early in spring, and larvae feed on algae and other aquatic vegetation. Adult salamanders feed on practically anything that moves, including other salamanders.

Unlike frogs or toads, salamander larvae have gills on the back of their heads. The gills look a little like feathers or tiny bushes.

For Further Information: <u>A Frog is Born</u>, William White Jr., Sterling Publishing Company.

THE LIFE CYCLE OF A NEWT

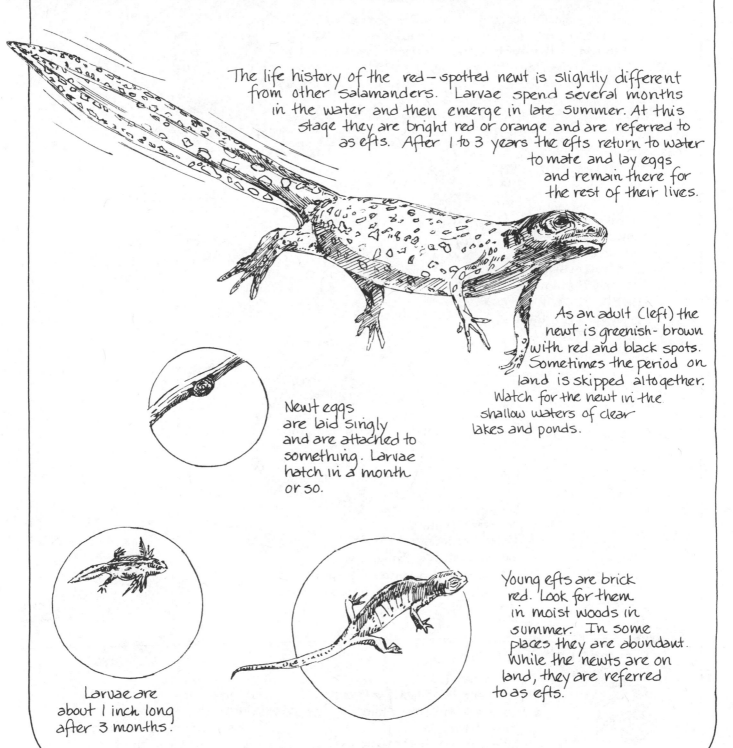

The life history of the red-spotted newt is slightly different from other salamanders. Larvae spend several months in the water and then emerge in late summer. At this stage they are bright red or orange and are referred to as efts. After 1 to 3 years the efts return to water to mate and lay eggs and remain there for the rest of their lives.

As an adult (left) the newt is greenish-brown with red and black spots. Sometimes the period on land is skipped altogether. Watch for the newt in the shallow waters of clear lakes and ponds.

Newt eggs are laid singly and are attached to something. Larvae hatch in a month or so.

Young efts are brick red. Look for them in moist woods in summer. In some places they are abundant. While the newts are on land, they are referred to as efts.

Larvae are about 1 inch long after 3 months.

For Further Information: <u>Reptiles and Amphibians</u>, Herbert S. Zim and Hobart M. Smith, Golden Press.

Water Insects

About 5,000 species of insects spend at least part of their lives in water spring is the best season to look for them. Smaller illustrations are about life-size.

Adult mayflies appear in late spring or summer. Some adults live only a few hours.

Look for stoneflies around streams in early spring. They have clear wings and long antennae.

Diving beetles are some of the more common aquatic insects. Some species trap a bubble of air and carry it beneath the surface for an extra supply of oxygen.

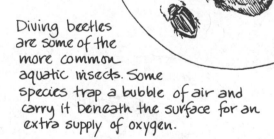

Water boatmen feed on vegetation. They swim with their rear legs, like a rowboat, sometimes carrying along a film of air.

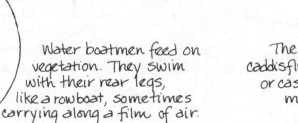

The larvae of caddisflies live inside tubes or cases made of sand or plant material. Look for them on stream bottoms.

For Further Information: <u>In Ponds and Streams</u>, Margaret Waring Buck, Abingdon Press.

Butterflies

Butterflies, like wildflowers and birds, each appear in certain seasons. Here are some of the ones you can expect in spring.

Mourning Cloak:
(early April)

Rich brown wings with a bright yellow border. The first butterfly to appear in spring.

Cabbage:
(early May)

White wings with dark tips on the fore-wings. Can be a pest on garden crops.

Sulphur:
(early to mid-May)

Yellow wings with dark borders.

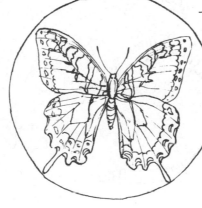

Tiger Swallowtail:
(last week of May)

Look for the "tails" on the wings. Yellow with tiger-like bands.

Wood Satyr:
(latter part of May)

Brown wings with black spots surrounded by a yellow ring. Look for satyrs in wooded areas.

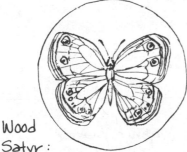

Spring Azure:
(3rd week of April)

Appears shortly after the mourning cloak. A small butterfly with pale blue wings.

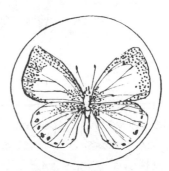

For Further Information: <u>Butterflies and Moths</u>, Mitchell and Zim, Golden Press.

WHAT LIVES IN THE SOIL

Below are some of the insects and invertebrates you can expect to find in soil. Some of these help to create healthy soil. Others, like the wireworm, may be harmful to garden plants.

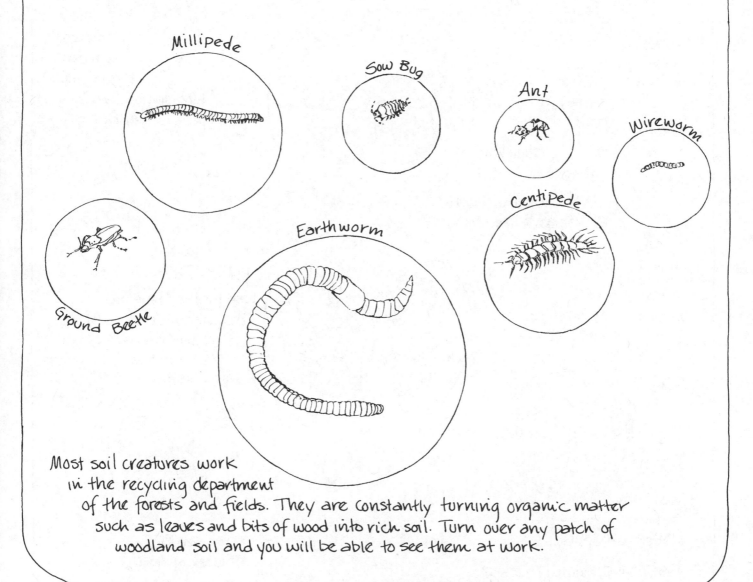

Millipede

Sow Bug

Ant

Wireworm

Ground Beetle

Earthworm

Centipede

Most soil creatures work in the recycling department of the forests and fields. They are constantly turning organic matter such as leaves and bits of wood into rich soil. Turn over any patch of woodland soil and you will be able to see them at work.

For Further Information: <u>Soil Animals</u>, Frederick Schaller, University of Michigan Press.

Woodland Wildflowers

Some of the most beautiful wildflowers
of the year blossom in the woods in spring
before the tree leaves come out.

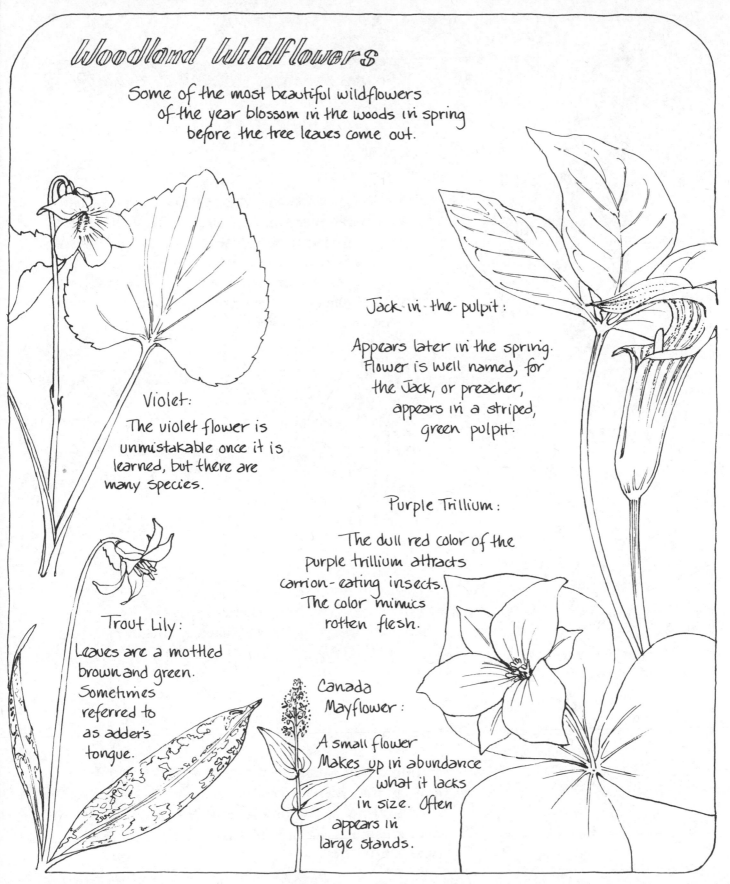

Jack-in-the-pulpit:

Appears later in the spring.
Flower is well named, for
the Jack, or preacher,
appears in a striped,
green pulpit.

Violet:

The violet flower is
unmistakable once it is
learned, but there are
many species.

Purple Trillium:

The dull red color of the
purple trillium attracts
carrion-eating insects.
The color mimics
rotten flesh.

Trout Lily:

Leaves are a mottled
brown and green.
Sometimes
referred to
as adder's
tongue.

Canada Mayflower:

A small flower
Makes up in abundance
what it lacks
in size. Often
appears in
large stands.

For Further Information: _Newcomb's Wildflower Guide_, Laurence Newcomb,
Little, Brown & Company.

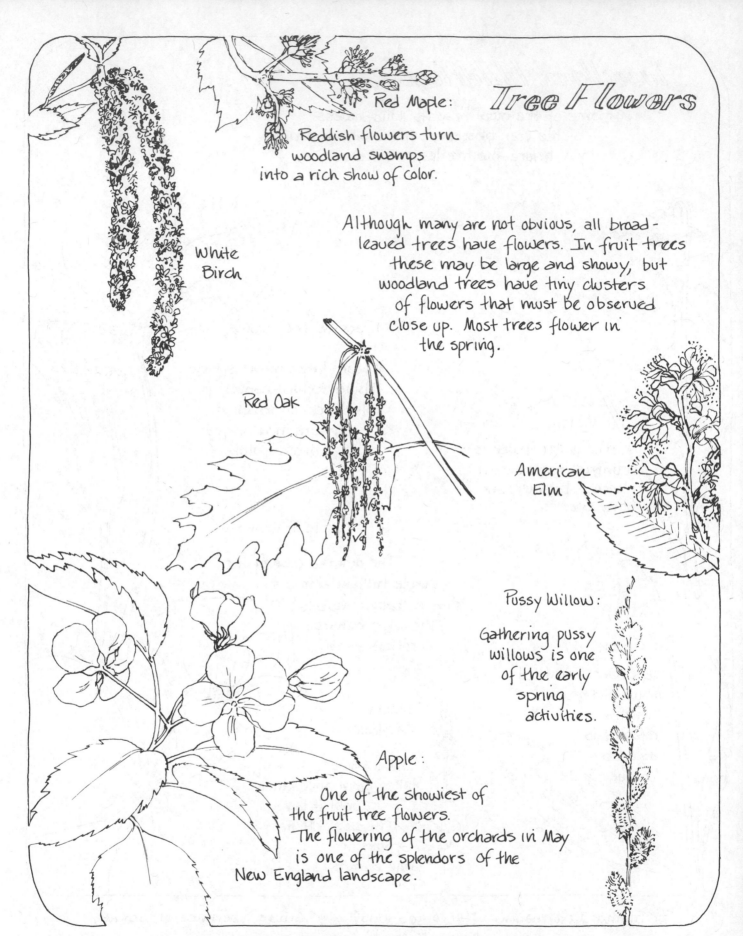

Red Maple:

Reddish flowers turn
woodland swamps
into a rich show of color.

Tree Flowers

White
Birch

Although many are not obvious, all broad-
leaved trees have flowers. In fruit trees
these may be large and showy, but
woodland trees have tiny clusters
of flowers that must be observed
close up. Most trees flower in
the spring.

Red Oak

American
Elm

Pussy Willow:

Gathering pussy
willows is one
of the early
spring
activities.

Apple:

One of the showiest of
the fruit tree flowers.
The flowering of the orchards in May
is one of the splendors of the
New England landscape.

For Further Information: The Blossom on the Bough, Anne Ophelia Dowden, Crowell.
Trees Flowers, Walter C. Rogers, Dover.

COMMON SHRUBS IN SPRING

Many of the shrubs which are buried in a confusion of green leaves in summer stand out brilliantly during the flowering of spring.

Early in spring the gray fuzzy catkins, or flowers, of the pussy willow appear. Later in spring and early summer the flowers develop into a long lacy fruiting body. (Left above.)

Watch for the long drooping catkins of speckled alder in swamps and wet areas. One of the most common wetland shrubs.

The shadbush blooms in May when the shad move up the rivers.

The brilliant red stems of the red osier are particularly obvious in early spring. The plant flowers later in the season in May or June.

Watch for the flowering of the viburnums late in May. There are many different species in North America.

For Further Information: <u>The Shrub Identification Book</u>, George W. D. Symonds, M. Barrows and Company.

Quaker-ladies

Bluets, or Quaker-ladies, bloom in mid-April in open fields or lawns. You will not find them listed in books on edible or useful plants. But the delicate beauty of these flowers has made them popular with naturalists throughout history.

Flowers grow on the ends of upright branches, or stems. There are four slightly pointed petals.

Quaker-ladies are pollinated by bees and small butterflies such as the painted lady or clouded sulphur.

The color of Quaker-ladies varies. Flowers in bright open areas may be pale blue or even white. Those in shady conditions are blue. Color variation may depend on acidity of soil as well as on light conditions.

Patches of Quaker-ladies sometimes cover large sections of a field or lawn. Sometimes they can be mistaken for patches of melting snow. Quaker-ladies do well in poor soil. They are often used in rock gardens.

For Further Information: <u>How to Know the Wild Flowers</u>, Mrs. William Starr Dana, Dover Publications.

GRASSES, SEDGES, RUSHES AND REEDS

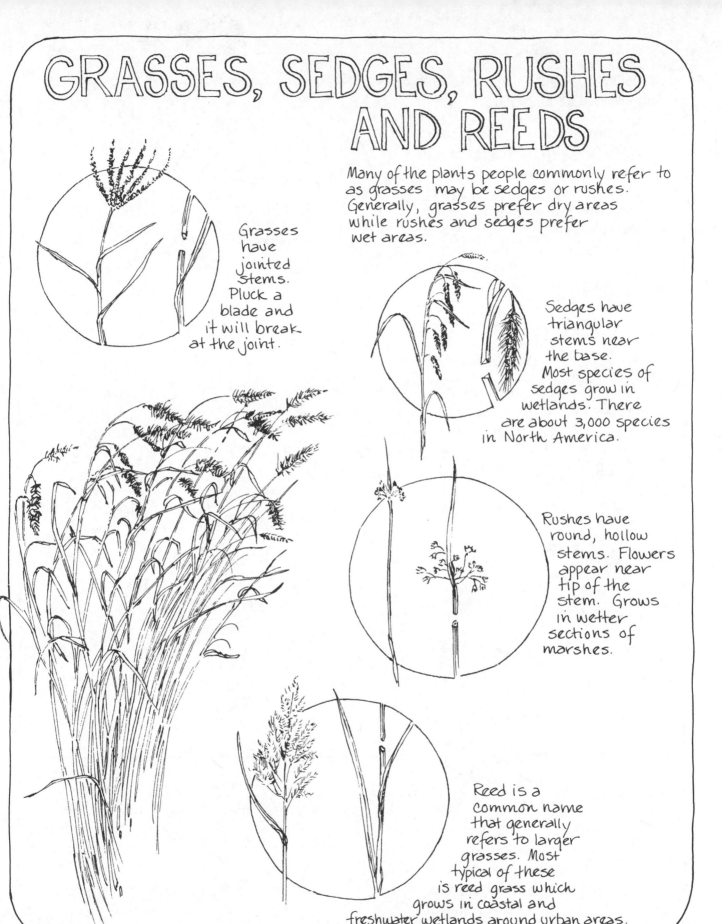

Grasses have jointed stems. Pluck a blade and it will break at the joint.

Many of the plants people commonly refer to as grasses may be sedges or rushes. Generally, grasses prefer dry areas while rushes and sedges prefer wet areas.

Sedges have triangular stems near the base. Most species of sedges grow in wetlands. There are about 3,000 species in North America.

Rushes have round, hollow stems. Flowers appear near tip of the stem. Grows in wetter sections of marshes.

Reed is a common name that generally refers to larger grasses. Most typical of these is reed grass which grows in coastal and freshwater wetlands around urban areas.

For Further Information: <u>Pond Life</u>, George K. Reid, Golden Press.

Wild Greens

Certain greens, when picked early in spring, make delicious additions to salads. In the past, wild greens provided the first fresh food after the winter.

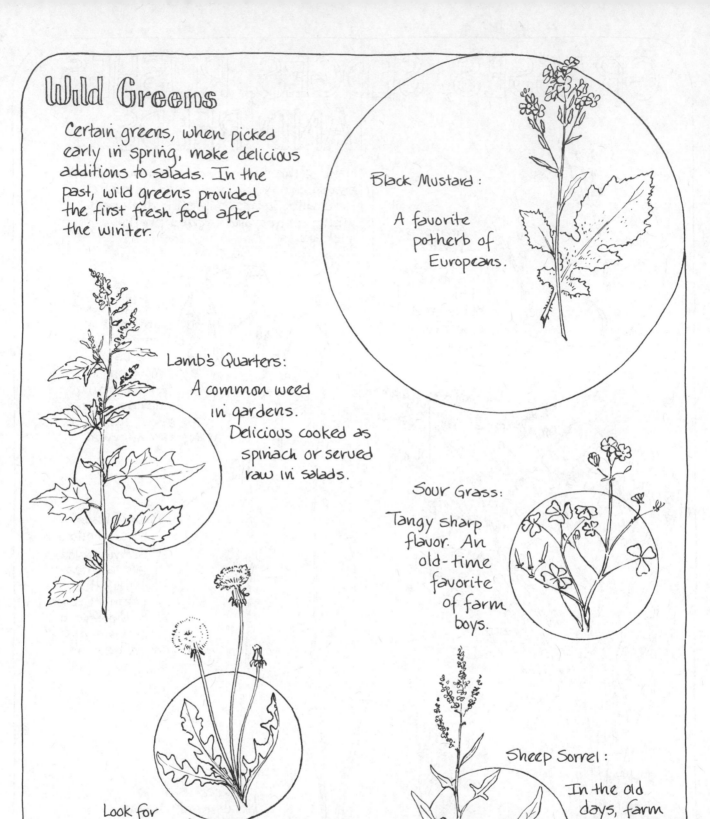

Black Mustard:

A favorite potherb of Europeans.

Lamb's Quarters:

A common weed in gardens.
Delicious cooked as spinach or served raw in salads.

Sour Grass:

Tangy sharp flavor. An old-time favorite of farm boys.

Look for the toothed leaves.
The name dandelion is from the French <u>dents de leon</u> — teeth of the lion.

Dandelion

Sheep Sorrel:

In the old days, farm wives used sheep sorrel as a rennet in cheese making.

For Further Information: <u>Stalking the Wild Asparagus</u>, Evell Gibbons, David McKay Co., Inc.

backyard sanctuary

You can encourage wildlife to visit your backyard by planting certain trees, shrubs, and herbaceous plants around your property. Or you can allow what is already there to go wild.

Leave dead trees standing. Woodpeckers and other species of birds rely on dead trees for nest holes.

Try to establish all types of plant communities on your property—old and young trees, shrubby areas and uncut sections of lawn.

For Further Information: _How to Invite Wildlife into Your Backyard_, David A. Herzog, Great Lakes Living Press.
Invite Wildlife to Your Backyard, National Wildlife Federation.

backyard sanctuary (cont.)

On this page are some of the trees and shrubs you might plant. They can be obtained through local nurseries or garden catalogs. Be sure to follow the particular planting instructions for each tree. Tree and shrub planting is an act of faith in the future. It also provides shelter and food for wildlife.

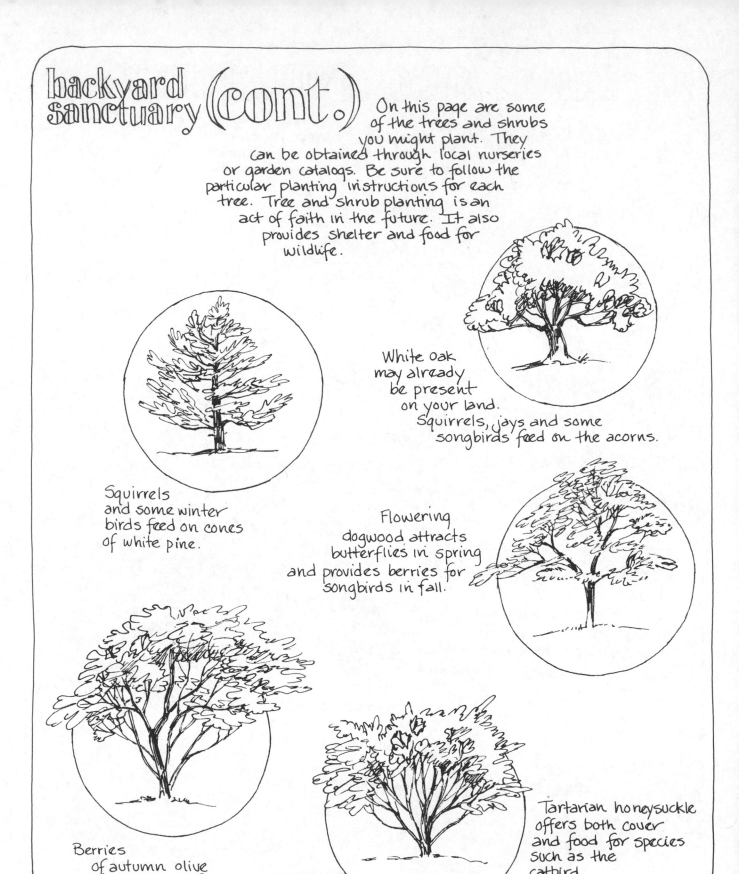

White Oak may already be present on your land. Squirrels, jays and some songbirds feed on the acorns.

Squirrels and some winter birds feed on cones of white pine.

Flowering dogwood attracts butterflies in spring and provides berries for songbirds in fall.

Berries of autumn olive provide excellent food for migrating birds.

Tartarian honeysuckle offers both cover and food for species such as the catbird.

For Further Information: <u>How to Invite Wildlife into Your Backyard</u>, David Alan Herzog, Great Lakes Living Press.

PLANTING FOR PROTECTION

Although the theory is still in the experimental stage, some agriculturalists believe that by careful arrangement of the plantings in your garden you can reduce insect damage. Here is a garden plan to follow. Strong-smelling herbs are believed to play an important role in insect control.

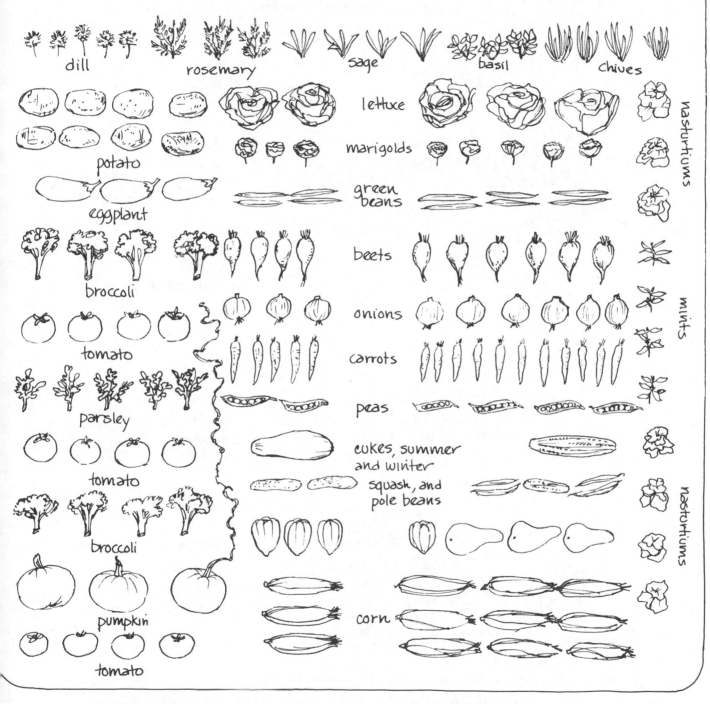

dill   rosemary   sage   basil   chives

potato   lettuce   marigolds   nasturtiums

eggplant   green beans

broccoli   beets

tomato   onions   mints

parsley   carrots

tomato   peas

cukes, summer and winter   squash, and pole beans   nasturtiums

broccoli

pumpkin   corn

tomato

For Further Information: <u>Companion Plants & How to Use Them,</u>
Philbreck & Gress, Devin, Adair.

WHEN TO PLANT

One of the arts of gardening is knowing when to plant what. You can tell when it is safe to plant the different garden crops by watching for the blooming of wild and domestic plants around your neighborhood. However, this system does not always work — sometimes nature is tricked by freak snowstorms or late frosts.

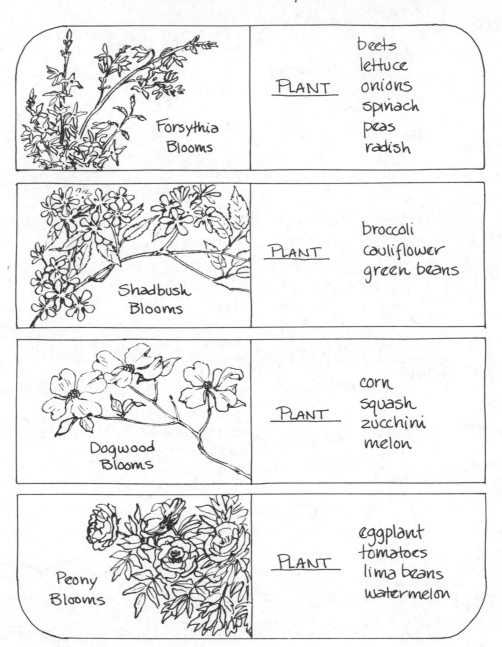

Forsythia Blooms

PLANT   beets
         lettuce
         onions
         spinach
         peas
         radish

Shadbush Blooms

PLANT   broccoli
         cauliflower
         green beans

Dogwood Blooms

PLANT   corn
         squash
         zucchini
         melon

Peony Blooms

PLANT   eggplant
         tomatoes
         lima beans
         watermelon

For Further Information: <u>The Basic Book of Organic Gardening</u>, Robert Rodale, Rodale Press.

Squashes and Gourds

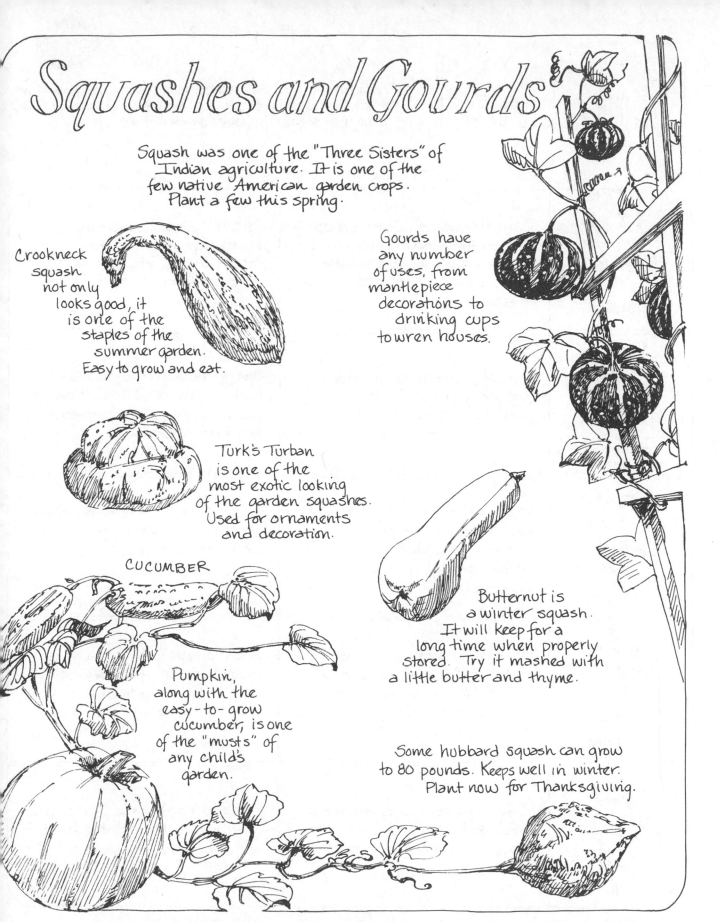

Squash was one of the "Three Sisters" of Indian agriculture. It is one of the few native American garden crops. Plant a few this spring.

Gourds have any number of uses, from mantlepiece decorations to drinking cups to wren houses.

Crookneck squash not only looks good, it is one of the staples of the summer garden. Easy to grow and eat.

Turk's Turban is one of the most exotic looking of the garden squashes. Used for ornaments and decoration.

CUCUMBER

Butternut is a winter squash. It will keep for a long time when properly stored. Try it mashed with a little butter and thyme.

Pumpkin, along with the easy-to-grow cucumber, is one of the "musts" of any child's garden.

Some hubbard squash can grow to 80 pounds. Keeps well in winter. Plant now for Thanksgiving.

For Further Information: <u>Backyard Vegetable Garden</u>, Hugh Wiburg, Exposition Press.

Herb Chart

Throughout history herbs have been grown for uses in medicine, magic, and food flavoring. Try growing some in your garden this spring.

	How To Grow	Uses
Parsley	Plant from seed in short rows in well-drained soil. Later can be divided. Does well in window boxes and small spaces. Slow to sprout.	One of the most common flavorings. Use in salads, eggs, or with meat, etc. Has been cultivated for at least 2,000 years.
Sweet Basil	Annual. Plant in rows after danger of frost. Cut for use as soon as the flowers open.	One of the staples of Italian dishes. The perfect addition to garden fresh sliced tomatoes. Dry for winter use.
Chives	No garden is complete without at least one clump of chives. Easy to grow from seedlings available at garden supply stores and nurseries.	Use in salads, with eggs, and especially with cottage cheese and cream cheese.
Spearmint	Plant from seedlings or root cuttings. Does well in sun or shade. Watch out for mints. They sometimes try to take over the garden.	A cup of spearmint tea on a bitter winter afternoon can cure a lot of miseries. Also good in homemade iced tea.
Dill	Plant from seed after danger of frost, in full sun. Cut leaves as needed. Let a few plants go to seed.	Dill and homemade pickles are inseparable, but try the herb with fish, and in salads.

For Further Information: <u>Companion Plants & How to Use Them</u>, Philbrick & Gress, Devin, Adair.

MAKE A BERLESE FUNNEL

You can get a good idea of what lives in soil by constructing a simple Berlese Funnel. The funnel operates by driving the moisture-loving soil insects away from heat and light. You will need the following things:

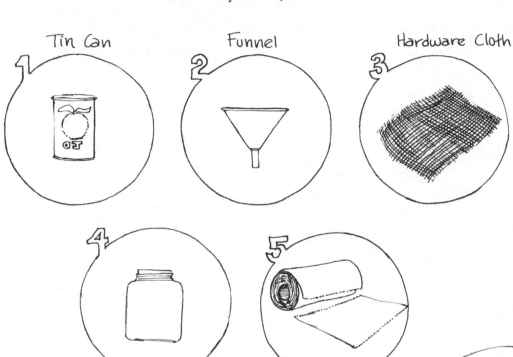

Tin Can

Funnel

Hardware Cloth

Jar

Paper Towel

Open both ends of the can, fill it with soil, and set it on the funnel on top of the hardware cloth. Set the funnel in full sunlight or under an electric light. The soil animals should tunnel deeper into the soil and fall through to the moistened paper towel on the bottom of the jar. Try soil from different habitats— woodlands, gardens, lawns, etc.

For Further Information: <u>Soil Animals</u>, Frederick Schaller, University of Michigan Press.

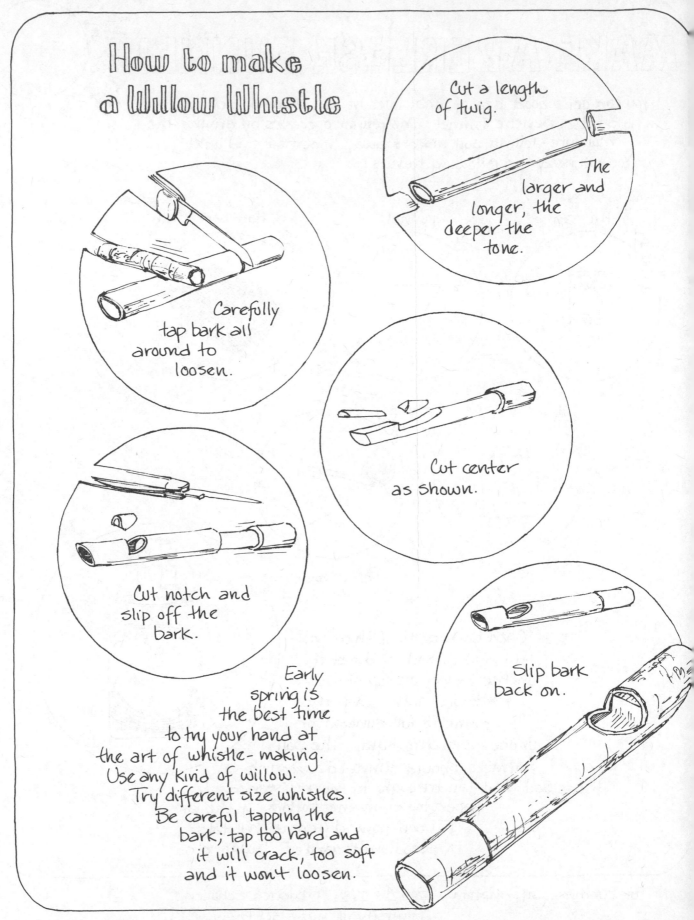

How to make a Willow Whistle

Cut a length of twig.

The larger and longer, the deeper the tone.

Carefully tap bark all around to loosen.

Cut center as shown.

Cut notch and slip off the bark.

Slip bark back on.

Early spring is the best time to try your hand at the art of whistle-making. Use any kind of willow. Try different size whistles. Be careful tapping the bark; tap too hard and it will crack, too soft and it won't loosen.

For Further Information: Easy Crafts, Ellsworth Jaeger, The Macmillan Co.

MAKE A TWIG BELT

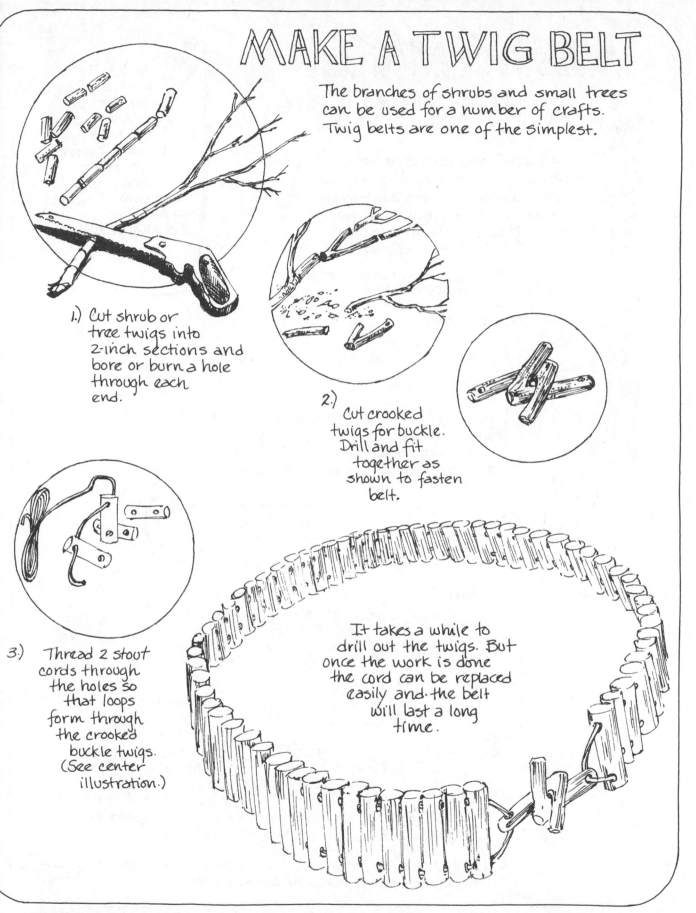

The branches of shrubs and small trees can be used for a number of crafts. Twig belts are one of the simplest.

1.) Cut shrub or tree twigs into 2-inch sections and bore or burn a hole through each end.

2.) Cut crooked twigs for buckle. Drill and fit together as shown to fasten belt.

3.) Thread 2 stout cords through the holes so that loops form through the crooked buckle twigs. (See center illustration.)

It takes a while to drill out the twigs. But once the work is done the cord can be replaced easily and the belt will last a long time.

For Further Information: <u>Nature Crafts</u>, Ellsworth Jaeger, The Macmillan Company.

HOW TO MAKE A RUSH MAT

Europeans and early American settlers used to spread rushes or sedges on their floors and sweep them out later when they got dirty. Pioneers also used to weave rushes into mats and rugs.

NOTE: THE MOST COMMONLY USED "RUSH" IS <u>SCIRPUS</u> <u>AMERICANUS</u>, THE CHAIRMAKER'S RUSH. THE PLANT IS ACTUALLY A SEDGE.

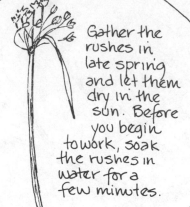

Gather the rushes in late spring and let them dry in the sun. Before you begin to work, soak the rushes in water for a few minutes.

Tie the ends of three rushes together and braid them together. Weave in new rushes as you work so that you make one long rope as shown in the lower illustration.

Weave in new strands as the rushes taper.

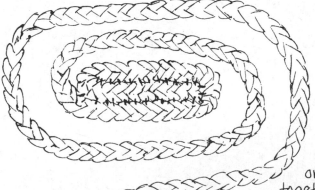

Coil the long braided rope. As you coil, sew the edges together with strong thread, or tie the edges together so that the knots will be on the underside of the mat. Rushes are useful plants so gather more than you think you need. The dried leaves can be used anytime to make woven mats or even baskets.

For Further Information: <u>Nature Crafts</u>, Ellsworth Jaeger, The Macmillan Company.

How To Make An Aquarium

You may want to keep some of the insects or amphibian larvae you find. Aquariums can be purchased or made from large jars or jugs. A small air pump should be used to keep the aquatic environment healthy.

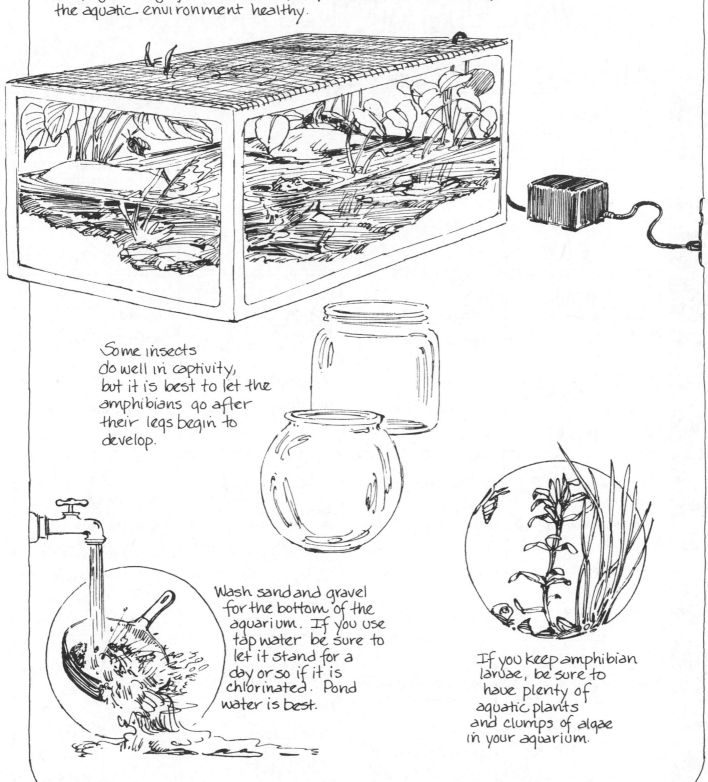

Some insects do well in captivity, but it is best to let the amphibians go after their legs begin to develop.

Wash sand and gravel for the bottom of the aquarium. If you use tap water be sure to let it stand for a day or so if it is chlorinated. Pond water is best.

If you keep amphibian larvae, be sure to have plenty of aquatic plants and clumps of algae in your aquarium.

For Further Information: <u>Enjoying Nature with Your Family</u>, Michael Chinery, Crown Publishers, Inc.

A CALENDAR OF NATURAL EVENTS

MONTH	1st week	2nd week	3rd week	4th week
MARCH				Skunk cabbage well up. Blackbirds, robins and song sparrows have returned. Shoots of day lily up.
APRIL	Wood frogs call. Salamander migration. Mourning cloak butterflies. Red maples bloom in swamps. Pussy willows out.	Spring peepers call. Tree swallows return. Phoebes. Forsythia blooms.	Spring azure butterflies. Toads call. House wrens. Spicebush blooms.	Catbirds. Swifts and barn swallows. Birch catkins out. Quaker-ladies bloom.
MAY	Black-and-white warblers. Yellow-rumped warblers. Dogwoods flower. Shadbush out. Violets bloom.	Warbler migration. Rose-breasted grosbeaks. Tanagers. Columbine blooms. Bloodroot flowers in open woods.	Indigo buntings. Great crested flycatchers. Lilacs bloom. Dandelions out. Buttercups.	Wood pewees. Flycatchers. Apple trees flower. Canada may flowers bloom.
JUNE	Young mammals leave nests. Wild geraniums and viburnums bloom.	First brood of young birds leave nests. Ox-eye daisy. Orange hawkweed.	First cutting of hay. Day lily flowers. Partridgeberries. Lady's slipper.	

Summer

As far as celestial events are concerned, winter, fall, and spring each have constellations that appear in the night sky to mark the season. Summer has one too; by late spring a huge triangle created by the bright stars, Altair, Vega, and Deneb, will appear overhead around ten o'clock and will remain visible throughout summer and well into fall. But unlike the other seasons the true symbol of summer rightly belongs to another celestial body, the nearby star that astronomers call the sun.

Summer is no season of slanting light and short days. More than anything else this time of year is dominated by the overwhelming presence of the sun. In some parts of the country, on June 21, the first day of summer, the earth and soil may still be cool and there may be any number of plants that have yet to fully develop.

Still, you have but to step outside some clear afternoon in late June and put your face up to the sky to feel the incredible force of heat coming from our nearest star. There will be hotter days as the summer season progresses, but on the twenty-first of June the rays of the sun will be striking the earth at the most direct angle, and it is this angle that generates the heat you feel.

It is of course the heat from the sun that is the source of all life on earth and serves as the fuel for the engines of the season. And it is now in late June that one of the most basic links in the complex chain of life gathers its sustenance as plants grow and blossom and the all-important work of photosynthesis begins.

Food chains and battles for survival notwithstanding, the process of growth creates a splendid show. June above all is the month of flowering plants. Deep in cool acid bogs, orchids such as arethusa, rose pogonia, and grass pink are in full bloom. In the open fields and pastures, black-eyed Susans, yarrow, and Indian paintbrush are flowering, and in deep woods, ferns such as the wood ferns, the cinnamon fern, and the ladyfern have unfurled their lacy fronds. Whatever is not in fruit or flower is at least in full leaf; and everywhere the woods and fields seem fresh. These are the weeks before the insect populations hatch, and the new leaves of trees and herbaceous plants are still undamaged. Later in the summer, within a few weeks of the beginning of the season, whole nations of leaf miners, leaf rollers, caterpillars, and similar herbivorous insects will hatch out and begin their work. Sometime toward late August, although the tree itself will not necessarily be damaged in any way, the full leaves of the June trees will be pierced and tunneled with the insects' work.

But all that is two months away. Now, early in the season, the plant world is at an apex. It is now that the first succulent cuttings of hay are made in rural areas. Roadside shrubbery is in the flush of first bloom, and in home gardens, peas are fattening in their pods, the first cutting of broccoli is ready, and the full leaves of spinach plants may just now begin to bolt in the hot sun.

As always, the bounty of the harvest may be tempered somewhat by a different sort of blossoming. The brief respite of full leaf will soon be over in the summer woods; late June and July mark the beginning of the hatching of the insects. Throughout the woods and fields the

hordes of eggs and pupae that were deposited on plant stems, twigs, and bark during the last days of the previous summer slowly begin to crack and split, and the nation of the insects begins to emerge. Everywhere during the early part of July, the world is alive with flying, burrowing, or crawling forms. There are times on summer nights when there seems to be no respite from them; they are ever-present, crawling up plant stems, resting under leaves, flying through the air, or rising in waves as you walk through long grass. Sometime during the course of the summer, every leaf of every tree, every blade of grass in the hay fields or wild meadows will serve as food, shelter, or resting place for some species of insect. There is no place that is free from them.

There is a strong tendency among the human community to complain about the hordes of insects that appear during the summer. More often than not they are the targets of both public and private eradication programs, most of which are temporary measures at best, and the majority of which are devastating to any number of innocent species. The fact is, a relatively small percentage of the insects that appear in summer have a negative effect on domestic plants. It has been calculated that some 98 percent of all insect species are either beneficial or benign and some of them—a great number of them if you happen to be interested in natural history—provide pleasure.

Typical of the latter type is the butterfly. During June and July and through August, the slow trickle of butterfly hatchings that began back in early spring with the small spring azure will burst into flood, as sulphurs, fritillaries, viceroys, monarchs, painted ladies, and swallowtails, each in their appointed season, burst from their pupae to flit across the summer meadows. At best, their season is short-lived. Although butterflies will grace the landscape from April through October, in general the individual lives of these fragile insects are measured in days or weeks. Some species do not even feed. They hatch, mate, lay eggs, and die; there is no time for the luxury of food.

More enduring, and in some ways no less beautiful, are the slim-bodied dragon-flies; summer is their season too. One by one as the warm weather progresses, the individual species emerge from ponds and streams as larvae, metamorphose, breed, and die. However, unlike the but-terflies, dragonflies are voracious pred-ators in all stages of their development. Most species spend at least one season as larvae on pond or stream bottoms actively seeking out smaller prey. Some night dur-ing the course of the summer, the water-dwelling larva will crawl out of the water onto a plant stem. Slowly, as the night progresses, the skin will dry and crack, and it will molt for the last time as a larva. At dawn the airborne adult will be darting over the marshes and meadows, leaving the dried husk of its past clinging to the stem.

The fact that such a common element of the summer landscape should spend the better part of its life in water is entirely fitting for the season. Much of summer seems to have something to do with water in one form or another. There are days early in the season when the entire atmosphere seems to be infused with moisture. In some areas, of course, it is the high humidity that ensures such a

lush blossoming. And not surprisingly, it is during the moist days of early summer that amphibians such as the frogs and salamanders desert the ponds where they were hatched and take to the woods and fields in search of food. Leopard frogs and pickerel frogs spring before you as you walk through damp meadows. On rainy afternoons in June and July, back roads in rural areas may be alive with red efts, the land stage of the newt, and in woods during the day spotted and red-backed salamanders emerge from their moist sanctuaries beneath rocks and logs to feed. On certain days when the tem-perature conditions are right, the woods may seem alive with wood frogs, and at night in gardens squat-bodied toads go about their work, devouring innumerable insect pests.

Everywhere in lakes and ponds, turtles, adult bullfrogs, green frogs, and the fat tadpoles of bullfrogs appear. Exposed rocks and logs at pond edges may be crowded with turtles, sometimes layered one atop the other in an attempt to achieve their place in the sun. Water snakes patrol the stream and pond edges, ribbon snakes slither along streams and through marshes. The venomous cop-perheads desert the high ledges of their wintering grounds and move to dank marshes. It is above all a season for cold-blooded species, such as the insects and the reptiles and the amphibians. All things that love the sun are out-of-doors in this season, feeding and foraging, and breeding.

But summer's lease has all too short a date. No sooner has the full flower of the season blossomed than one by one the stops of the great seasonal engine begin to close down. And typically, the fourth season, late summer, goes out in splendor—nature seems to revel in great exits. It is now, towards the end of August, that the full chorus of insects reaches its height as katydids, long-horned grasshoppers, snowy tree crickets, and meadow crickets liven the late summer nights with their music. The sun may be slowly weakening in the western sky and the lush grasses of early summer may be dry and brown on the hillsides, but in the fields and backyards the night may be nearly deafening with the racket of insects.

The loud energetic nights are in sharp contrast to the days. There are times at midday from late July to mid-August when the woods may seem as still as they were in January. A walk in some nearby forest will reveal little more than a few gnats and perhaps a languorous fly or two. Life is in a sort of temporary estivation, waiting for the cooler hours of dusk and predawn. Throughout the woods and fields, mammals and birds are in secluded resting places, and nowhere is the crowd of summer life to be seen. There is only one sound that may be apparent in the summer woods, and that is the lazy call of the red-eyed vireo repeating its endless chant from the canopy of the forest—"Going up. Going down. Going up. Going down."

These are the easy days, the so-called dog days, named for the Dog Star, Sirius, by the Egyptians, who believed the rays of the star combined with the sun to create the heat of summer. But like the summer itself, the dog days are short-lived. The days end earlier, and late summer nights may be chill. Even before summer officially ends on the twenty-first of September there will be a few killing frosts in the summer gardens in northern areas, and slowly, night by night, the great triangle of summer, as well as the nearby star, the sun, will rise later and later and set earlier and earlier.

The Summer Sky

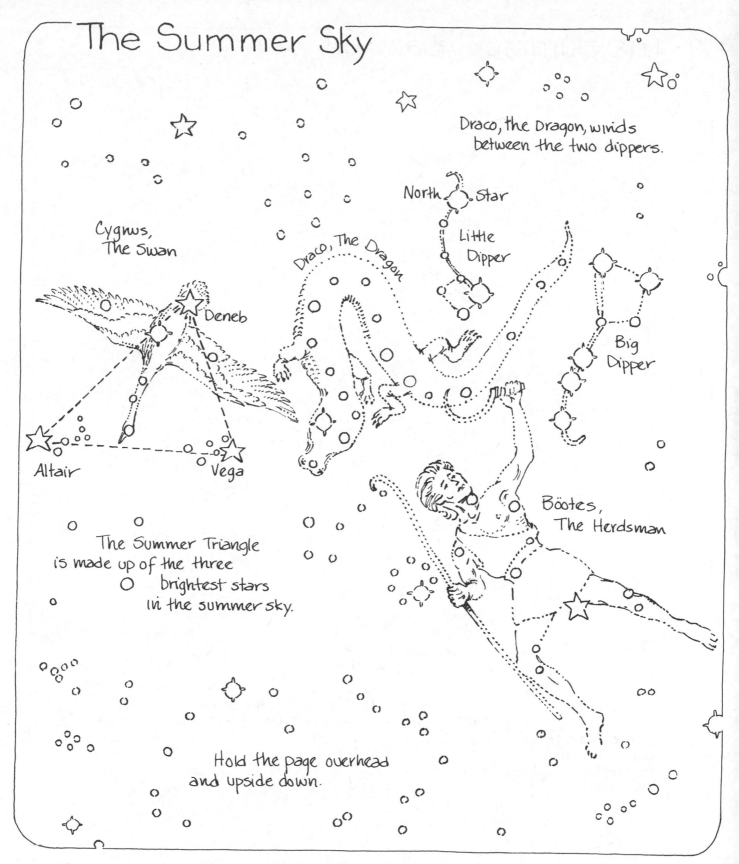

Draco, the Dragon, winds between the two dippers.

North — Star

Little Dipper

Big Dipper

Cygnus, The Swan

Draco, The Dragon

Deneb

Böotes, The Herdsman

Altair

Vega

The Summer Triangle is made up of the three
O brightest stars in the summer sky.

Hold the page overhead and upside down.

For Further Information: <u>Find the Constellations</u>, H. A. Rey, Houghton Mifflin.

The Summer Triangle

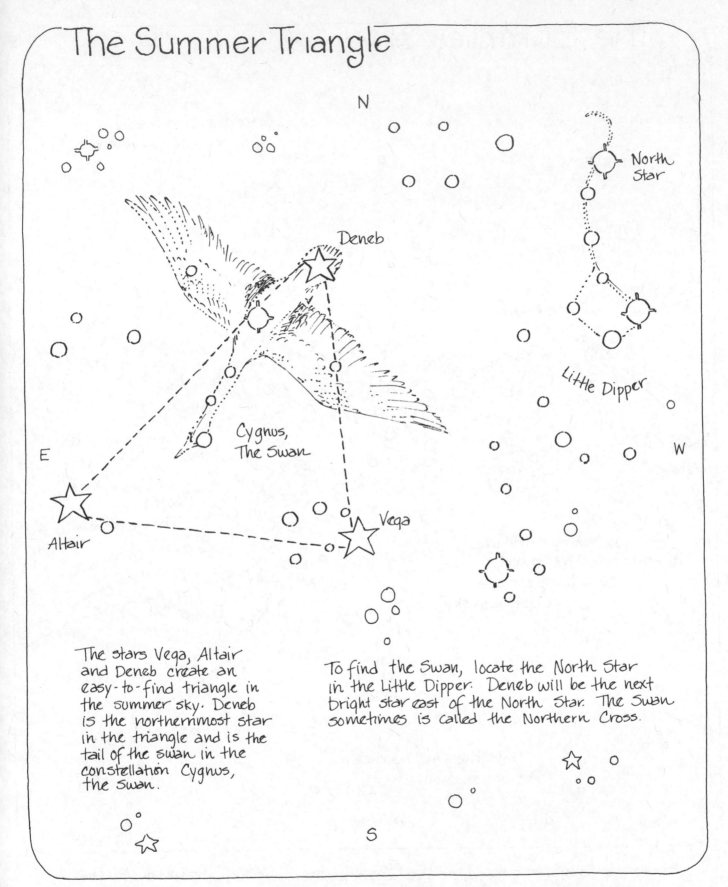

N

North Star

Deneb

Little Dipper

E

Cygnus, The Swan

Altair

Vega

W

S

The stars Vega, Altair and Deneb create an easy-to-find triangle in the summer sky. Deneb is the northernmost star in the triangle and is the tail of the swan in the constellation Cygnus, the Swan.

To find the Swan, locate the North Star in the Little Dipper. Deneb will be the next bright star east of the North Star. The Swan sometimes is called the Northern Cross.

For Further Information: <u>Find the Constellations</u>, H. A. Rey, Houghton Mifflin.

The Summer Swallows

Swallows are a sort of poor man's barometer. On damp or windy days, they fly low over the fields to get the tiny insects that make up their diet. But when it is hot and fair, they fly high above the fields among the clouds.

Bank Swallows:

Look for the brown band across the breast and the white throat. Bank swallows nest in colonies in river banks and gravel pits. The adults work in shifts, pecking the sand and gravel loose so they can scratch out a burrow with their feet.

Rough-winged Swallows:

Common near water. Watch for the brown back and the brown throat. Sometimes dip into the water as they feed.

Barn Swallows:

Nest in barns and old buildings. Common in rural areas. The only swallow with a deeply-forked tail.

Tree Swallows:

Common around suburban yards. Can be told from other swallows by its bright green back. Tree swallows are the first swallows to arrive in spring and the last to leave in autumn.

For Further Information: <u>A Field Guide to the Birds</u>, Roger Tory Peterson, Houghton Mifflin.

LIFE IN THE SUMMER SKY

Summer life is so rich, it even crowds itself into the sky.

DAYTIME **EVENING**

Nighthawks are common over cities. They nest on the flat roofs of buildings. Watch for the long, pointed wings, and the erratic, turning flight.

Tree Swallow: Dark green back, whitish underparts.

During the last week in August, nighthawks begin to migrate south in a wide front that extends all the way across the North American Continent.

Chimney Swift: Looks like a cigar with wings. Swifts often circle around nesting chimneys in huge, swirling hoardes.

The Little Brown Bat: Common over back yards in the evening. Try throwing a small stone in the air near them. They will dive for it. They are most active in the hour after sunset and the hour before sunrise.

Barn Swallow: Forked tail.

For Further Information: <u>How to Know the Birds</u>, Roger Tory Peterson, New American Library.

BIRD FEATHERS

A walk in the woods in summer will probably turn up a few bird feathers. Identify them, but don't take them home. There is a federal law against keeping feathers.

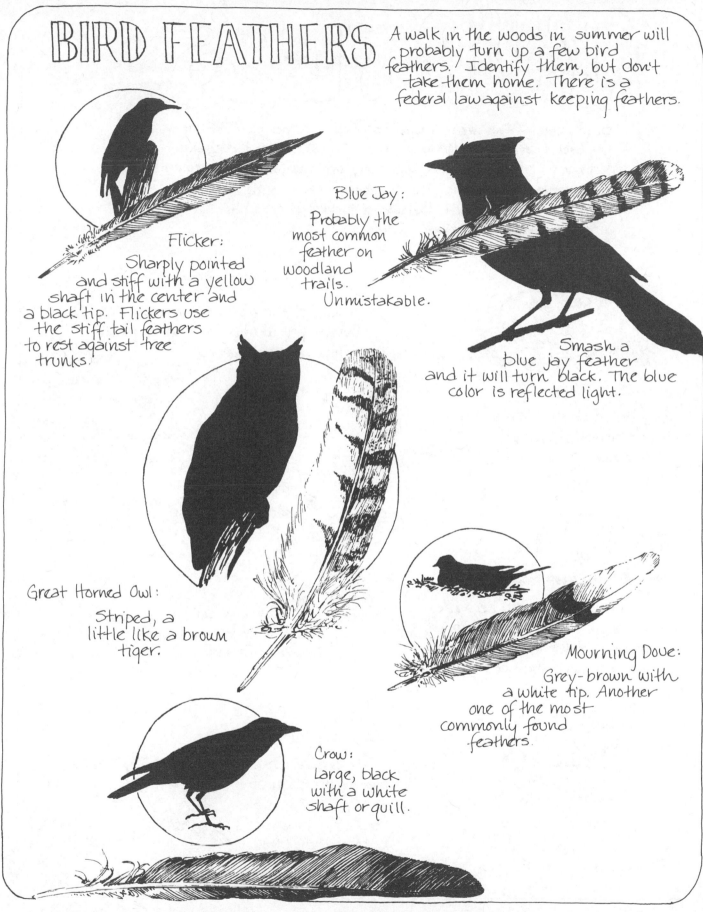

Flicker:
Sharply pointed and stiff with a yellow shaft in the center and a black tip. Flickers use the stiff tail feathers to rest against tree trunks.

Blue Jay:
Probably the most common feather on woodland trails.
Unmistakable.

Smash a blue jay feather and it will turn black. The blue color is reflected light.

Great Horned Owl:
Striped, a little like a brown tiger.

Mourning Dove:
Grey-brown with a white tip. Another one of the most commonly found feathers.

Crow:
Large, black with a white shaft or quill.

For Further Information: <u>Watching Birds, An Introduction to Ornithology,</u> Roger F. Pasquier, Houghton Mifflin.

TURTLES

Surely one of the great tragedies of environmental destruction is the fact that in the Northeast, many populations of turtles are declining. Turtles, like man, generally are omnivorous — they eat both plants and animals. Turtle decline is due to habitat destruction and pollution. But use of turtles for pets has upset populations of certain species.

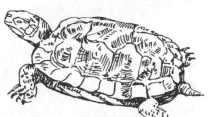

Painted Turtle:

One of the more common species. Bright yellow and red edge on shell. They often bask on exposed logs.

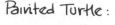

Wood Turtle:

Gray-brown, shaped like a Chinese helmet. Wood turtles are declining and are even rare in some areas.

Box Turtle:

Declining, partly because people take them for pets. Leave box turtles alone in the woods where they belong.

Musk Turtle:

Common, but rarely seen. Most of time spent under water.

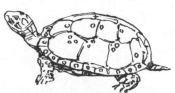

Spotted Turtle:

Also declining. They lay only 2 to 3 eggs per year. Black, with yellow spots.

Snapping Turtle:

Snappers are scavengers, part of the clean-up crew of ponds. Generally their hiss is worse than their bite. A fine turtle.

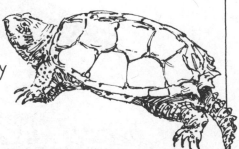

For Further Information: A Field Guide to Reptiles & Amphibians of Eastern & Central North America, Roger Conant, Houghton Mifflin.

SNAKES

Milk Snake:

Found on farms and around stone walls where it hunts mice and other small rodents. Often mistaken for the copperhead.

Ringneck Snake:

Common in forested areas. Feeds entirely on salamanders. Small, 1 to 1½ feet in length.

Snakes are one of the most colorful parts of any landscape. They are most active in summer, but are sometimes commonly found along sun-warmed, black-topped roads in fall. Snakes in northern areas hibernate in winter, sometimes balled together in a huge tangle.

Black Racer:

Large, sometimes up to 6 feet. Found in open country near marshes and swamps. Feeds on frogs and rodents. Watch out — although harmless, black racers are quick to bite.

Garter Snake:

Perhaps the best-known snake. Feeds on earthworms, salamanders and frogs.

Brown Snake:

Common in suburban and even backyards, cities. Eats slugs and earthworms. Small, 1 foot.

Water Snake:

Found in streams and ponds. Feeds on frogs and slow-moving fish. The poisonous cottonmouth, for which this species is mistaken, is not found in northern areas.

For Further Information: <u>Reptiles and Amphibians</u>, Herbert S. Zim & Hobart M. Smith, Golden Press.

THE GARTER SNAKE

Often referred to as the grass snake, the garter snake is probably the most commonly seen snake in the United States.

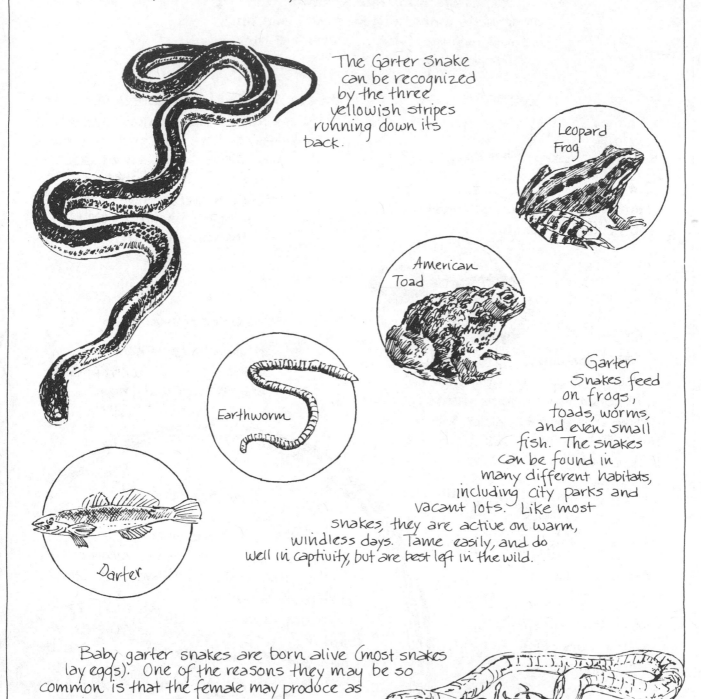

The Garter Snake can be recognized by the three yellowish stripes running down its back.

Leopard Frog

American Toad

Earthworm

Garter Snakes feed on frogs, toads, worms, and even small fish. The snakes can be found in many different habitats, including city parks and vacant lots. Like most snakes, they are active on warm, windless days. Tame easily, and do well in captivity, but are best left in the wild.

Darter

Baby garter snakes are born alive (most snakes lay eggs). One of the reasons they may be so common is that the female may produce as many as 50 young a year.

For Further Information: <u>Field Book of Snakes</u>, Schmidt and Davis, Putnam, 1941.

LIFE ON A LOG

One of the best areas in which to experience the rich variety of life on the woodland floor is in a fallen tree or limb. Many of the living things you will find, such as the mosses and lichens, are breaking down the log into soil. In fact, inside the log, you might find the soil already has been made.

Lady Fern

The white oblong things you see in ants nests are larvae, not eggs. If you happen to disturb the nest, the ants will scurry to save the larvae.

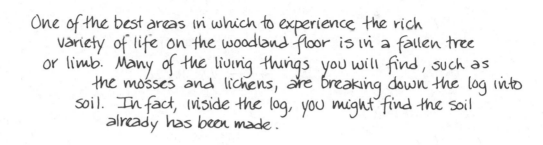

Pin Cushion Moss

Ant larvae

Pixie-cup Lichen

Pale-shield Lichen

Red-backed Salamander:

Sometimes can be found in logs, in the moist center of decayed wood.

For Further Information: <u>Questions and Answers About Ants,</u> Millicent E. Selsom, Scholastic Book Services.

LIFE UNDER A ROCK

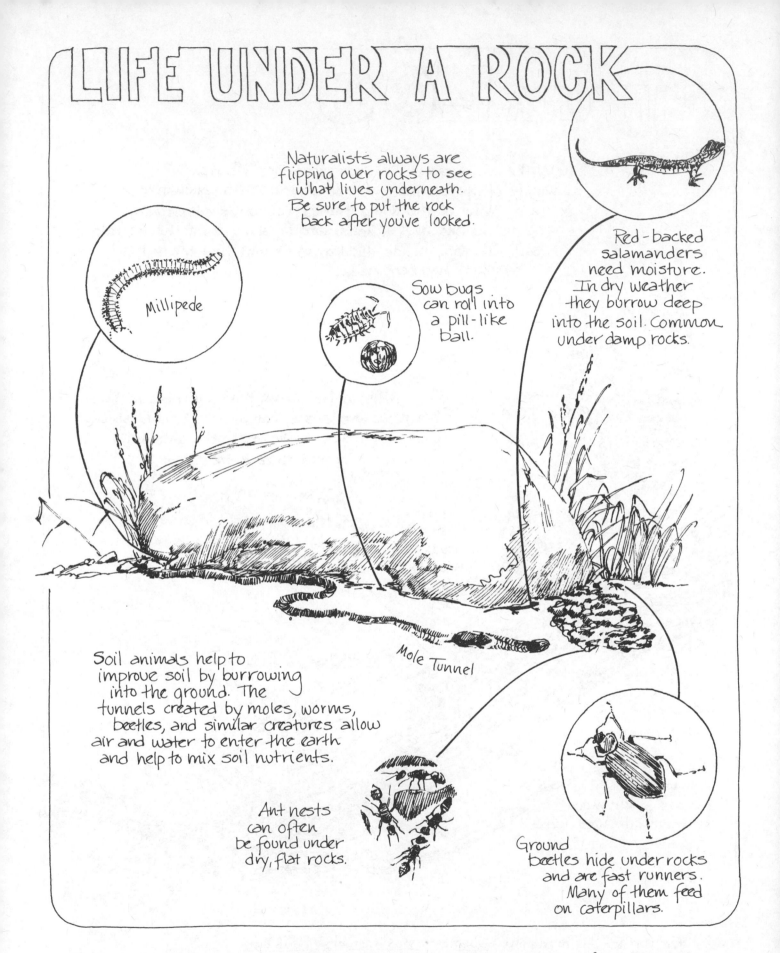

Naturalists always are flipping over rocks to see what lives underneath. Be sure to put the rock back after you've looked.

Millipede

Sow bugs can roll into a pill-like ball.

Red-backed salamanders need moisture. In dry weather they burrow deep into the soil. Common under damp rocks.

Mole Tunnel

Soil animals help to improve soil by burrowing into the ground. The tunnels created by moles, worms, beetles, and similar creatures allow air and water to enter the earth and help to mix soil nutrients.

Ant nests can often be found under dry, flat rocks.

Ground beetles hide under rocks and are fast runners. Many of them feed on caterpillars.

For Further Information : <u>Soil Animals</u>, Frederick Schaller, University of Michigan Press.

TENT CATERPILLARS AND FALL WEBWORMS

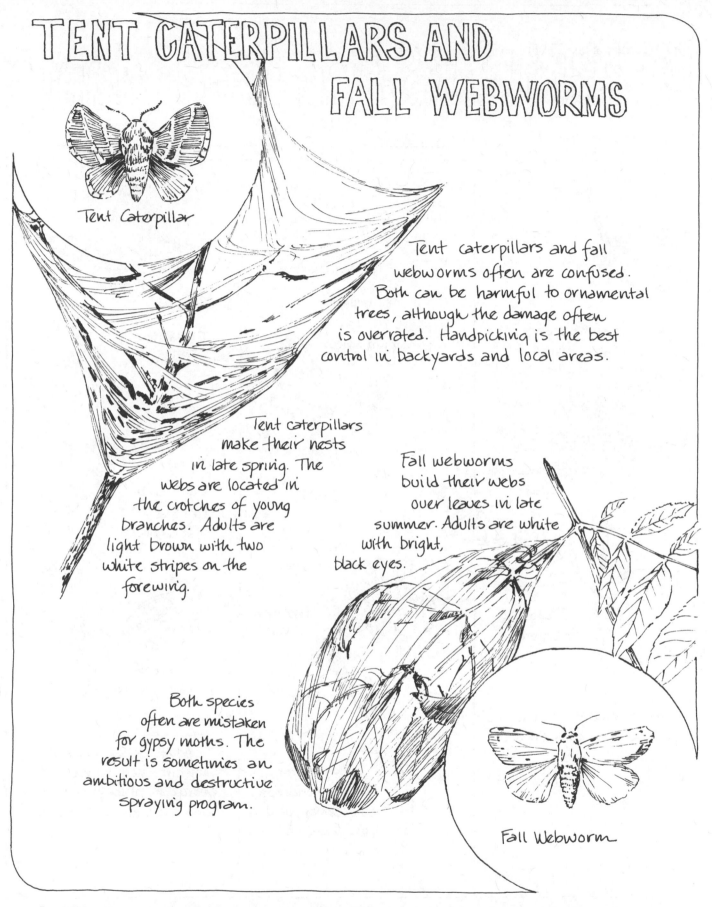

Tent Caterpillar

Tent caterpillars and fall webworms often are confused. Both can be harmful to ornamental trees, although the damage often is overrated. Handpicking is the best control in backyards and local areas.

Tent caterpillars make their nests in late spring. The webs are located in the crotches of young branches. Adults are light brown with two white stripes on the forewing.

Fall webworms build their webs over leaves in late summer. Adults are white with bright, black eyes.

Both species often are mistaken for gypsy moths. The result is sometimes an ambitious and destructive spraying program.

Fall Webworm

For Further Information: Man and Insects, L. H. Newman, Natural History Press.

CATERPILLARS and food plants

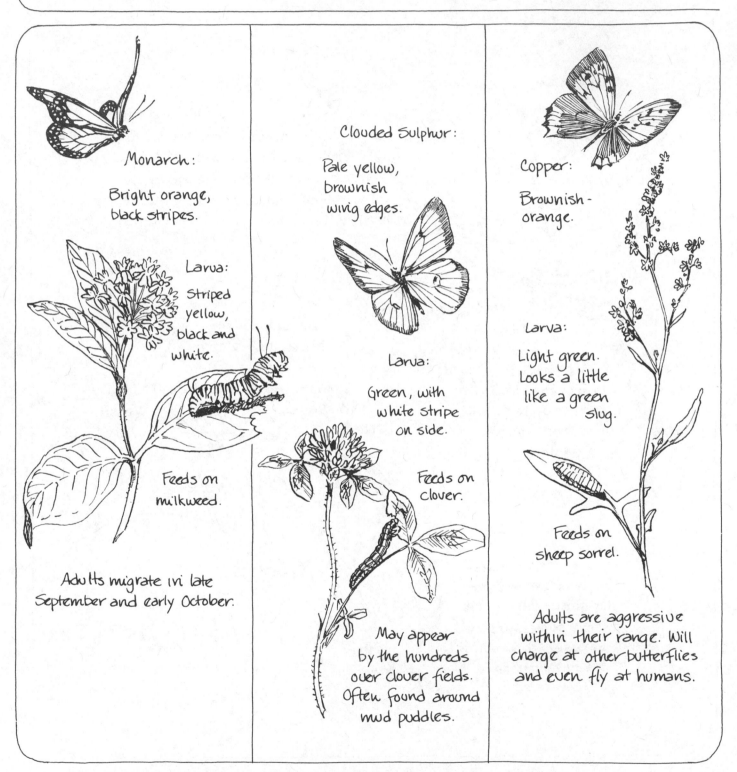

Monarch:

Bright orange, black stripes.

Larva:

Striped yellow, black and white.

Feeds on milkweed.

Adults migrate in late September and early October.

Clouded Sulphur:

Pale yellow, brownish wing edges.

Larva:

Green, with white stripe on side.

Feeds on clover.

May appear by the hundreds over clover fields. Often found around mud puddles.

Copper:

Brownish-orange.

Larva:

Light green. Looks a little like a green slug.

Feeds on sheep sorrel.

Adults are aggressive within their range. Will charge at other butterflies and even fly at humans.

For Further Information: _Field Book of Insects_, Frank E. Lutz, Putnam.

# of SUMMER BUTTERFLIES

Most butterfly larvae (caterpillars) feed and lay their eggs on specific plants.

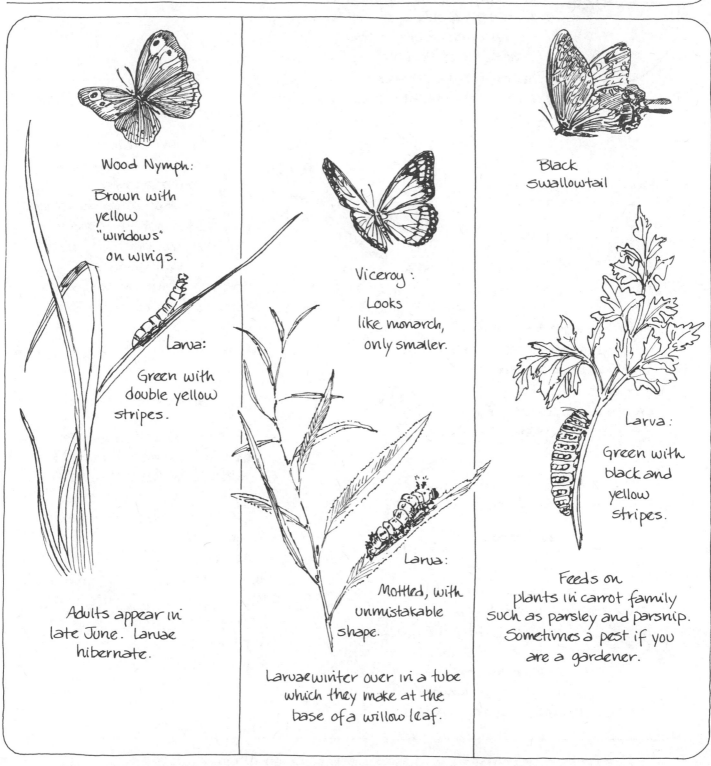

Wood Nymph:

Brown with yellow "windows" on wings.

Larva:

Green with double yellow stripes.

Adults appear in late June. Larvae hibernate.

Viceroy:

Looks like monarch, only smaller.

Larva:

Mottled, with unmistakable shape.

Larvae winter over in a tube which they make at the base of a willow leaf.

Black Swallowtail

Larva:

Green with black and yellow stripes.

Feeds on plants in carrot family such as parsley and parsnip. Sometimes a pest if you are a gardener.

For Further Information: <u>Field Book of Insects</u>, Frank E. Lutz, Putnam.

BACKYARD INSECTS DAY

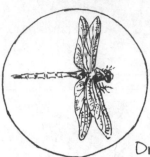

Green Darner:

One of the most common species of dragonflies, often seen hovering over open fields. They are one of the few insects that migrate. Dragonflies are predatory. They catch insects on the wing, like hawks.

Praying Mantis:

So called because of the position it assumes while resting and feeding. A predator on garden pests. Watch out; if handled, they can bite with their legs. Egg cases are sold in some garden supply shops as pest controls.

Ladybug:

Perhaps the best-known backyard insect. Also one of the most beneficial to gardeners. The larvae of ladybugs feed on aphids, a sometimes serious plant pest.

Carolina Grasshopper:

A large insect with black and yellow wings that flies up suddenly in front of you when you walk in tall grass. One of the most common grasshoppers and one of the easiest to identify — just get them to fly to see the wing pattern.

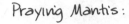

Leaf Hopper:

A small, green, bullet-shaped insect often found on garden plants. Like aphids, they suck plant juices, and can be harmful if there are too many of them. There are a number of brightly-colored species.

For Further Information: <u>Insects</u>, Herbert S. Zim, Golden Press.

NIGHT

Katydid:

A beautiful, jade-green grass-hopper-like insect. The katydid says its name again and again. The calls of katydids and snowy tree crickets are the most common sounds of the summer night.

Snowy Tree Cricket:

Rarely seen, but often heard. Call is a dull, whistle-like sound. Often call in unison, so that the night seems to throb. Unlike other crickets, climbs into shrubbery and tall flowers.

Crane Fly:

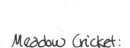

Looks like a huge mosquito, but feeds entirely on vegetation and does not bite. Generally found in wet areas.

A Cricket Thermometer:

Count the number of snowy tree cricket "throbs" in 13 seconds, add 40, and you will have the temperature within a few degrees Fahrenheit.

Meadow Cricket:

The light, tinkling sound you hear in the grass both day and night is the call of this common cricket.

June Bug:

Large, glistening brown beetle. This is the insect that hammers on screens on June nights. Sometimes considered a pest.

For Further Information: <u>A Dog's Book of Bugs</u>, Elizabeth Griffen, Atheneum.

insects in the grass

Sweep an insect net through the long grass like a broom a few times and you will scoop up a surprising variety of species.

(Drawings not to scale.)

Tortoise Beetle

Some species of tortoise beetles look like flat ladybugs or tiny turtles.

A jar with a net top will make it easy to observe the insects you will catch.

Short-horned Grasshopper

Probably the most common insect in the grass. Antennae of this grasshopper are always much shorter than the body.

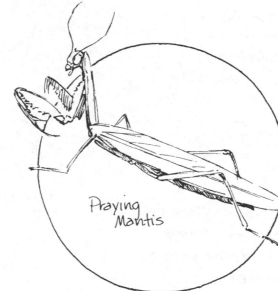
Praying Mantis

Young praying mantises are one of the common insects in grass in mid to late summer.

Stink Bug

If you disturb the stink-bug you will smell the reason for its name. Body brownish-green and shaped like a shield.

Red-banded Leafhopper

One of the most colorful insects in the grass, red-banded leafhoppers look like torpedo-shaped American flags.

For Further Information: <u>Field Book of Insects</u>, Frank E. Lutz, Putnam.

STINGING INSECTS

Try ice or cool mud to relieve the pain of bee stings. If abnormal swelling, shortness of breath or itching occurs, call a doctor. Allergic reactions to bee stings can be serious.

Bald-faced hornets have the worst sting. Nests are large and turnip-shaped. Usually hung from tree branches or roof peaks of old houses.

Yellow jackets are attracted to sweets and meat. They often nest around houses and can produce a nasty sting. Colonies die in winter and are reproduced again by the queen who hibernates for the season.

Except for the honeybee, colonies of bees and wasps die each year in the fall. They are repopulated in spring by the queens.

Paper wasps are more easy-going than some of the other insects on this page. Also, their stings are not as painful.

Bumblebees have a painful sting, but are usually less likely to use it. Like all stinging insects, the sting is pure defense — sometimes a last resort.

Honeybees are probably the most familiar and beneficial of all the bees and wasps. Honeybees die when they sting. The barbed stinger remains in the flesh along with the rear end of the bee. Colonies spend winter in the hive.

For Further Information: <u>A Bee Is Born</u>, Harold Doering, Sterling.

A Guide to Common Dragonflies

All dragonflies spend part of their lives in water. The larval stages feed voraciously on other aquatic insects. They climb onto stems of aquatic plants at night to molt into adult form.

Dragonflies rest with their wings out flat. The more delicate damselflies (above) fold their wings behind them.

Green Darner:

Largest of the dragonflies. Clear wings at least two inches long. Body and head bright green. Watch for them over fields in August. They are found in Asia and throughout the Western Hemisphere.

White-tail:

Common around ponds and ditches. Holds its wings forward slightly when resting. Watch for the broad, solid white tail.

Common Skimmer:

Common around ponds. Rests on tall grasses or branches and darts out after prey.

Sympetrum:

Easily recognized by their brilliant red bodies. Often found far from water.

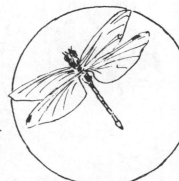

For Further Information: <u>Dragonflies and Damselflies</u>, Mary G. Phillips, Crowell.

ATTRACTING MOTHS

You can attract a number of different species of moths with a simple light trap.

To attract moths, build a "card house" of screens around an electric light, or tack an old sheet onto the side of the house and shine a bright light on it.

Watch for underwing moths at the light trap. Forewings have a dull pattern, under-wings are brightly colored.

NOTE:
Commercially sold black lights, which attract and then zap night-flying insects for the most part kill only the harmless species. Only two percent of the insect species are pests.

Moths have feathery antennae and generally fly at night.

Butterflies have thin antennae that end in a club and fly only during the day.

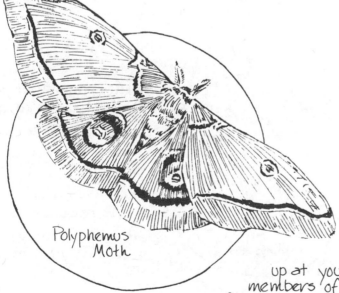

Polyphemus Moth

Without question, the most beautiful moths that will show up at your light trap will be members of the Saturnid family. These large, beautifully colored moths include the polyphemus, promethea, cecropia, luna, and io moths. Wingspread may be as much as six inches.

For Further Information: <u>Butterflies and Moths</u>, Mitchell & Zim, Golden Press.

HOW TO RAISE A MONARCH

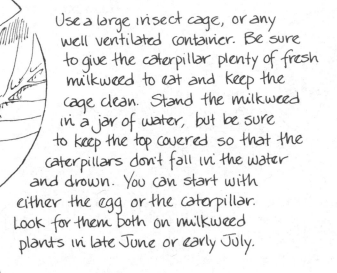

Use a large insect cage, or any well ventilated container. Be sure to give the caterpillar plenty of fresh milkweed to eat and keep the cage clean. Stand the milkweed in a jar of water, but be sure to keep the top covered so that the caterpillars don't fall in the water and drown. You can start with either the egg or the caterpillar. Look for them both on milkweed plants in late June or early July.

Newly hatched monarch drying its wings.

Egg

Larva

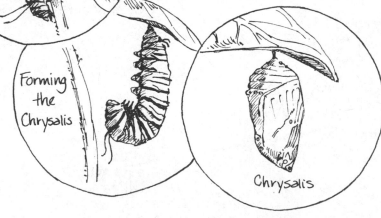

Forming the Chrysalis

Chrysalis

After two or three weeks, the caterpillar will crawl to the top of the cage and form a jade-green chrysalis. 12 to 15 days later, the monarch will hatch. Be sure to release the butterfly in the same area that you found it.

For Further Information: _A Field Guide to the Butterflies_, Alexander B. Klots, Houghton Mifflin.

TREE LEAVES WITH TEETH

Inspect tree leaves to see whether the leaves have teeth, or lobes, or have smooth edges. Here are some of the common toothed leaves.

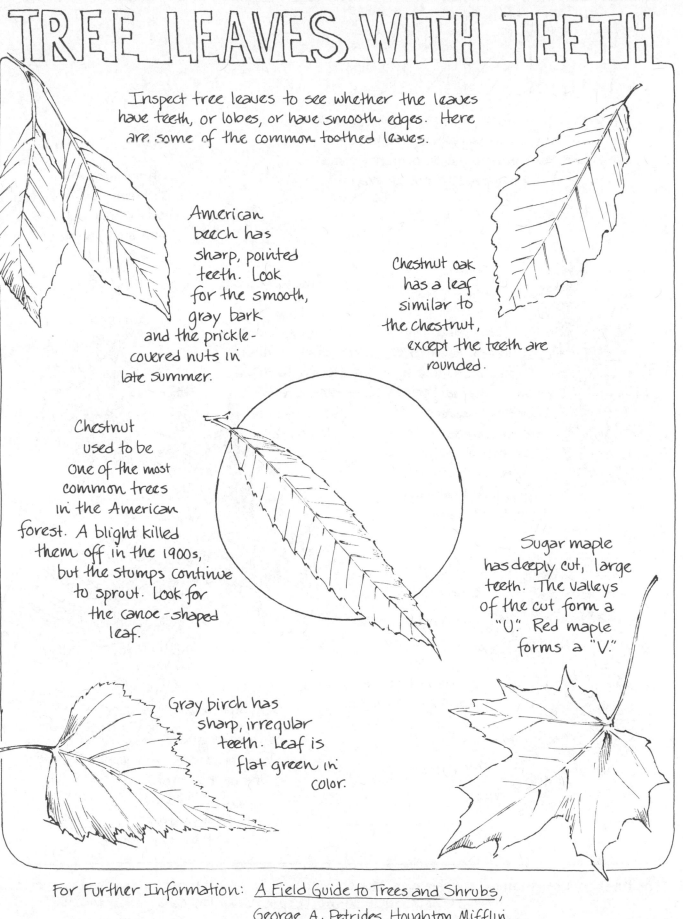

American beech has sharp, pointed teeth. Look for the smooth, gray bark and the prickle-covered nuts in late summer.

Chestnut oak has a leaf similar to the chestnut, except the teeth are rounded.

Chestnut used to be one of the most common trees in the American forest. A blight killed them off in the 1900s, but the stumps continue to sprout. Look for the canoe-shaped leaf.

Sugar maple has deeply cut, large teeth. The valleys of the cut form a "U." Red maple forms a "V."

Gray birch has sharp, irregular teeth. Leaf is flat green in color.

For Further Information: _A Field Guide to Trees and Shrubs,_ George A. Petrides, Houghton Mifflin.

FERNS

It takes seven years for a fern plant to mature. Ferns are non-flowering plants. In the age of the dinosaurs, they grew to the size of trees and were the dominant plant in the landscape.

Hay-scented Fern:

Has rich smell of fresh cut hay. Common in open glades and on roadsides.

Royal Fern:

Large and many leaves. Royal fern looks more like a shrub than a fern. Found in swamps and wet areas. Like many species of ferns, they are often found growing in large stands.

Cinnamon Fern:

Look for a cinnamon-colored stalk. This is the fruiting body of the fern — like the flower of flowering plants.

Bracken:

Three branching fronds, common in open woods and clearings in large stands.

Sensitive Fern:

Look for unique shape of leaves. One of the first plants killed by autumn frosts, thus the name.

For Further Information : _A Fern is Born_, Cuilcher E. Noailles, Sterling Nature Series. _A Field Guide to the Ferns_, Boughton Cobb, Houghton Mifflin.

CLUB MOSSES (LYGOPODEUMS)

Like ferns, club mosses are non-flowering plants. They are evergreen — some of them have the appearance of small evergreen trees. Look for them in deep woods. The fruiting body is borne on a separate stalk. It is now illegal to pick a number of species of club mosses. In the old days, people used to gather them for Christmas decorations and the plants were over-picked.

Shining Club Moss:

Like wolf's claw, but thicker, with sharp leaves.

Tree Club Moss:

Upright, like a small tree.

Wolf's Claw:

Upright, branched stems rising from a stem along the ground.

Running Ground Pine:

Thin, upright stems with tightly packed leaves.

For Further Information <u>Non-flowering Plants</u>, Frederick S. Shuttlesworth and Herbert S. Zim, Golden Press.
<u>Plants Without Leaves</u>, Ross E. Hutchins, Dodd, Meade and Company.

FIELD and ROADSIDE WILDFLOWERS

Black-eyed Susan

Some of the brightest flowers in the American fields were brought over from Europe with the colonists. Most of them grow in areas that have been altered, such as fields or roadsides. Native American flowers are more common in woodlands and natural meadows.

Butter-and-eggs:

Named for the two shades of yellow that appear in the flowers. Common in waste places.

Hawkweed:

Orange-red flowers, a recent migrant to this country.

Milkweed:

Pinkish ball-like heads.

Indian Paintbrush:

Brilliant deep reds.

Toadflax:

Blue flowers, slender spikes.

Daisy

Field and roadside flowers are the least appreciated of the wildflowers. They often fall victim to the mower, or worse, to roadside spraying programs.

For Further Information: _A Field Guide to Wildflowers_, Roger Tory Peterson and Margaret McKenny, Houghton Mifflin.

Edible Roots and Tubers

Spring is a time for edible wild greens, but summer is for roots and tubers — especially in late summer. Be sure to leave a few plants behind to restock your supply next year.

Chicory

Dry the roots of chicory, grind and use as a substitute for coffee.

Groundnut has vine-like stems and chocolate-colored flowers. Dig the tubers in late summer. Bake like a little potato.

Watch for the yellow flowers of Jerusalem artichokes in late summer. Roast or fry the tubers like a potato. Sold in supermarkets.

Burdock

The Japanese cultivate burdock for its edible root. Eat boiled, or use in Oriental dishes.

Cattail was an important food for the American Indians. Roots can be dried and ground into flour, or boiled.

Cattail

For Further Information: <u>Feasting Free on Wild Edibles</u>, Bradford Angier, Stackpole Books.

CLOUD WATCHING

There is no season like summer for watching the sky. It is then that the most interesting and varied cloud formations appear.

Cumulo-nimbus may rise to 75,000 feet.

Cumulus:

Fluffy white clouds with dark bases that usually mean fair weather. Sometimes pile up enough to bring rain showers.

Cumulonimbus:

Probably the most spectacular formation. Often bring thunderstorms.

Nimbostratus:

Heavy dark clouds that usually appear before rain or snow. Common in winter.

Cirrus:

Commonly referred to as "Mare's Tails." Cirrus clouds are created by tiny beads of ice. They are high-level clouds – 20,000 feet or more. The word "Cirrus" is from the Latin "to curl."

Stratocumulus:

Low, water-carrying clouds. Often threaten bad weather.

For Further Information: _Eric Sloane's Weather Book_, Eric Sloane, Hawthorn. _Instant Weather Forecasting_, Alan Watts, Dodd, Mead & Company.

SHOOTING STARS

Meteors, commonly called shooting stars, are stony particles from inter-stellar space that enter Earth's atmosphere. Friction from their high-speed entry causes them to burn up, thus creating the appearance of a shooting star.

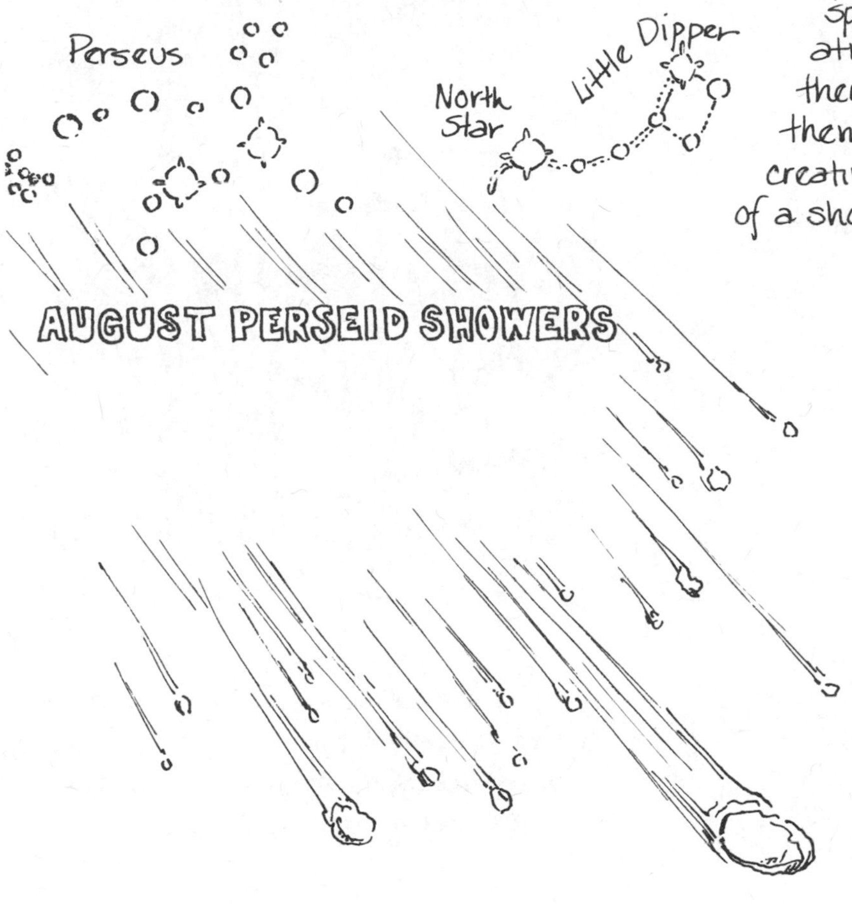

Perseus

North Star

Little Dipper

AUGUST PERSEID SHOWERS

Notice that by August, the Little Dipper has swung around from its early summer position.

Sometime in the middle of August, usually between the 10th and the 17th, there is a shower of meteors in the constellation Perseus in the northeastern part of the sky. The best showers appear after midnight, but many meteors can be observed earlier.

For Further Information: The Sky Observer's Guide, Newton R. Mayall, Golden Guide.

backyard sanctuary
make a weed garden...

You can create an interesting natural corner in your yard by turning over a section of lawn and allowing the weeds to take over. Many of the so-called "weeds" that will invariably appear offer the best food supply for winter birds and small mammals.

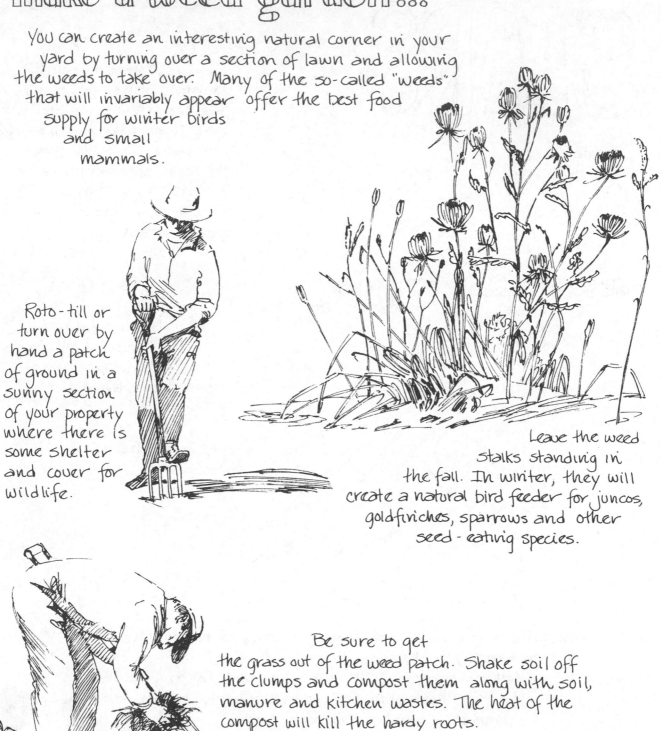

Roto-till or turn over by hand a patch of ground in a sunny section of your property where there is some shelter and cover for wildlife.

Leave the weed stalks standing in the fall. In winter, they will create a natural bird feeder for juncos, goldfinches, sparrows and other seed-eating species.

Be sure to get the grass out of the weed patch. Shake soil off the clumps and compost them along with soil, manure and kitchen wastes. The heat of the compost will kill the hardy roots.

For Further Information: _Science in Your Own Backyard_, Elizabeth K. Cooper, Harcourt, Brace & World, Inc.

WEEDS TO WATCH FOR

Within a week or so, the first weed seedlings will appear in your patch. Let them grow throughout the season — some will change form dramatically.

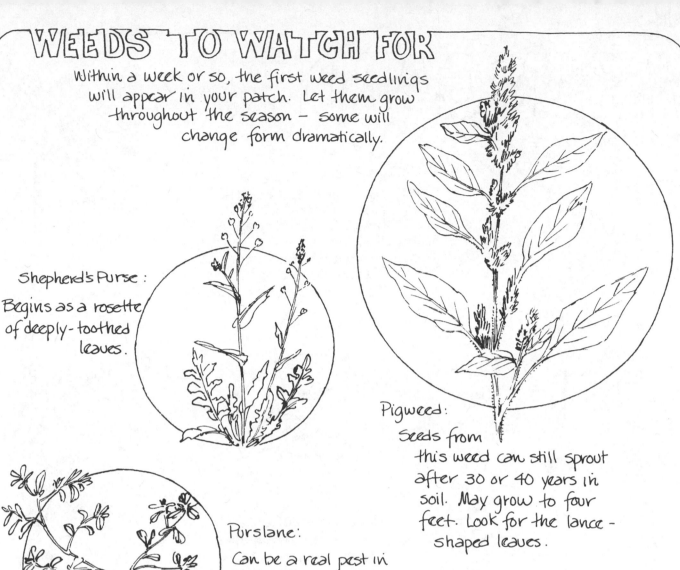

Shepherd's Purse :

Begins as a rosette of deeply-toothed leaves.

Pigweed:

Seeds from this weed can still sprout after 30 or 40 years in soil. May grow to four feet. Look for the lance-shaped leaves.

Purslane:

Can be a real pest in the vegetable garden. Thick, fleshy, rounded leaves.

Sheep Sorrel:

Probably the first weed to appear in your patch.

Lamb's Quarters:

Like many weeds, lamb's quarters was introduced from Europe. Try some young leaves in a salad.

For Further Information : <u>Weeds</u>, Alexander C. Martin, Golden Guide.

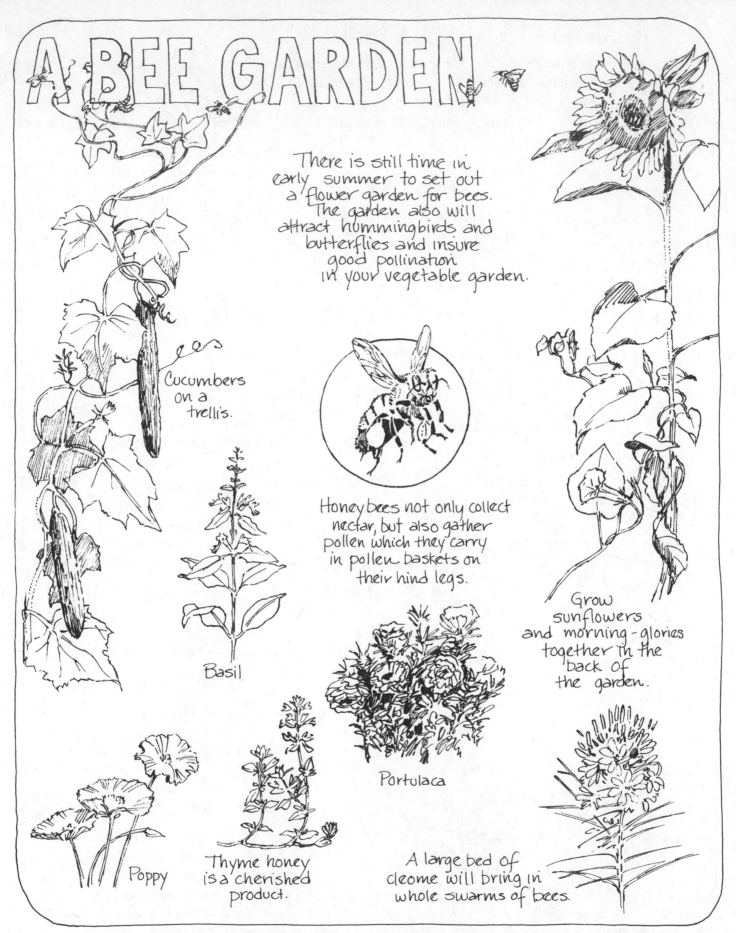

A BEE GARDEN

There is still time in early summer to set out a flower garden for bees. The garden also will attract hummingbirds and butterflies and insure good pollination in your vegetable garden.

Cucumbers on a trellis.

Honey bees not only collect nectar, but also gather pollen which they carry in pollen baskets on their hind legs.

Basil

Portulaca

Grow sunflowers and morning-glories together in the back of the garden.

Poppy

Thyme honey is a cherished product.

A large bed of cleome will bring in whole swarms of bees.

For Further Information: _Garden Annuals and Bulbs_, Anthony Huxley, Macmillan.

HOW TO MAKE AN INSECT CAGE

You can make a simple insect cage with two straight-sided cake pans and a swatch of window screening. Cut the screening to whatever height you need, sew the edges together and set this screen cylinder between the cake pans as shown.

Except for caterpillars, which you can feed with their preferred food plants, it is probably best to observe any insects you catch for a little while and then release them. Insects, like any wild thing, do not do well in captivity.

For caterpillars, set food plants in a jar of water. Force the stems through holes pierced in the cap, or stuff the top of the jar with rags. Caterpillars sometimes fall in the water and drown. Keep caterpillars supplied with fresh plants.

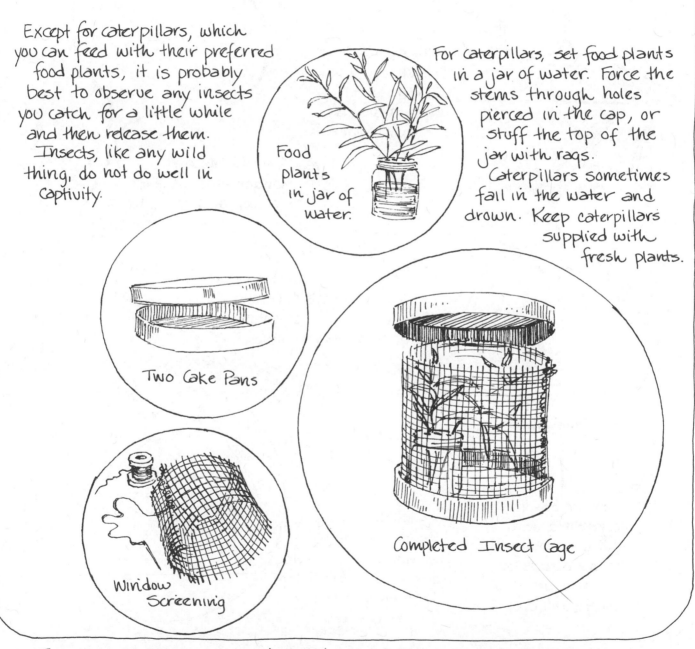

Food plants in jar of water.

Two Cake Pans

Window Screening

Completed Insect Cage

For Further Information: <u>Snips & Snails & Walnut Whales — Nature Crafts for Children</u>, Phillis Fiarotta, Workman Publishing Co.

how to make an insect net

A good, homemade insect net will help you explore the wildlife in the grassy jungle. You can use the net like a broom, sweeping through the lighter grasses to see what you come up with, or you can go after individual insects.

1. You will need a large swatch of muslin or mosquito netting and a wire coat hanger.

2. Unwind the coat hanger and bend it into a loop and straighten the ends.

4. Notch a heavy dowel or broomstick at one end as shown.

3 ft.

3. Sew or staple the netting onto the wire loop with the loose ends on the outside. Any shape will do.

5. Fit the straight ends into the notch and bind as tightly as you can with wire, tape or string. Strength is important.

For Further Information: <u>Man and Insects</u>, L. H. Newman, Natural History Press.

WHAT TO DO WITH ORPHANED WILDLIFE-
Mammals

The best thing you can do with apparently orphaned birds and mammals is leave them alone. In most cases, the parents are nearby. Adult animals can take care of their own young. Sometimes young are abandoned because the parents sense that their young will not survive because of some defect. There are certain situations, however, where a little human care can help.

```
MAMMAL FORMULA

1 part evaporated milk
1 part water
1 dash karo syrup
      SERVE WARM
```

Feed holding animal upright. Be sure to keep the formula out of animal's nose.

Uprooted Rabbit Nest:

Locate the nest and replace the young. If possible, keep cats and dogs away. The mother rabbit will return.

Squirrels or Tree Dwellers:

Feed with an eye dropper or dolls bottle every four hours throughout day and night. More frequently, if they have no fur.

Keep young in ventilated box which is placed on a heating pad. Call vet for injuries.

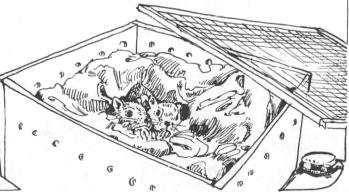

For Further Information: <u>Care of the Wild Feathered & Furred, A Guide to Wildlife Handling & Care,</u> Mae Hickman & Maxine Guy, Unity.
<u>The Quality of Mercy</u>, Charles E. Roth, Massachusetts Audubon Society.

WHAT TO DO WITH ORPHANED WILDLIFE-
Birds

Parent birds continue to feed their young after they leave the nest. There is rarely such a thing as a lost bird. Be sure to release any bird you raise as soon as its tail feathers develop.

The best thing you can do when you find any animal is to contact a local animal care center to get help. In most states it is illegal to keep mammals, and there is a federal law against keeping birds.

Birds with No Feathers:
Locate nest and replace the bird. Parents will continue to feed it, even if you have touched it. If you can't find the nest, line a berry box with dry grass and nail it to a tree where you found the bird.

Birds with No Tail Feathers:

Put the bird high in a nearby shrub, and do your best to keep cats and dogs away. The parent birds will continue to feed it.

For Injured Birds:

Call local animal care center. For emergency care, feed with mixture of moistened, canned dog food and hard-boiled egg.

For Further Information: <u>Care of the Wild Feathered & Furred, A Guide to Wildlife Handling & Care</u>, Mae Hickman & Maxine Guy, Unity Press.
<u>The Quality of Mercy</u>, Charles E. Roth, Massachusetts Audubon Society.

A CALENDAR OF NATURAL EVENTS

MONTH	1st week	2nd week	3rd week	4th week
JUNE	Toad tadpoles in shallow ponds. Daisy and yarrow bloom. Oriole nests at ends of elm branches.	Tiger swallowtail butterflies. Fireflies appear. Wood nymph butterflies.	Bats out in full force. Devil's paintbrush blooming in fields. Viceroy butterflies. June bugs.	Meadow crickets calling. First cutting of hay. Bullfrogs calling.
JULY	Paper wasp nests complete. Deer flies. Red admiral butterfly. 17-year locust calls.	Mullein in bloom. Day lily flowers. Gray tree frogs call. Monarch butterflies appear.	Chicory in blossom along roadsides. Indian pipes in deep woods.	Praying mantises abundant. Snowy tree cricket calls Katydids begin to call.
AUG.	Night chorus of insects in full swing. Barn swallows begin to gather on wires.	Burdock blooms. Perseid meteor showers in northeast sky, 10 p.m. Corn is ripe.	Early morning spider webs. First asters. Nighthawks pass.	Barn swallows leave. First wave of fall warbler migration. Fall webworms.
SEPT.	Tree swallow migration. Watch full moon for passing bird migrants.	Green darner migration. Goldenrods and asters in full bloom.	Monarch butterfly migration. Broad-winged hawks on the move. Apples ripe.	

FALL

It might be worthwhile for anyone interested in natural history to spend at least one night of the year under the open sky. Late summer is without doubt the best time to do it; the insects are for the most part gone, the air is still warm, and there is a lot of activity in the night sky in late August that is worth staying up for. In fact the show is spectacular enough to merit selecting a spot that offers you a clear view of the sky, even if that spot happens to be the rooftop of some city apartment. If you get to your place before dark, you may be able to see the first of the late summer events as flights of slim-winged birds slip past one after another. These are nighthawks, a species closely related to the whippoorwill, and each August they migrate south in a wide front that stretches all the way across the nation. Although they are common, this may be the only time you will see these night-flying birds.

Later in the evening, towards midnight and on through the night, if you watch the northeastern sector of the sky, you may be able to see a number of shooting stars. These are the remnants of the Perseid meteor showers that occur towards the middle of the month in the constellation Perseus. Even though the height of the shower period will have passed, late summer is generally a good season for meteors.

If you are ambitious, or wakeful just before dawn, you will notice a bright band of stars rising slowly in the east, silently, and with all the splendor that characterizes celestial events. This is the constellation Orion, and it is the first sign of the approaching winter.

Orion is the archetypal seasonal constellation; no other celestial formation accompanies its season with such brilliance. Orion will remain in the winter sky from early fall through the softening period of April when the streams run once more and the frogs begin to call. During the course of its passage across the sky, here on earth nature will be put to its severest test. Winter is the anvil upon which the ecology of the landscape is shaped.

Fortunately, there is time to prepare. The season between September and December, which we refer to as autumn, is above all a season for getting ready. Evolution has created a number of methods of dealing with the iniquities of winter, and fall is the time of year when these various systems begin to activate themselves. Certainly the simplest and the most dramatic of these is migration. Rather than face the problems of survival created by winter, in the best escapist tradition, birds and some insects simply fly away. This at once creates a spectacle and a mystery. Even after a century or more of theories, scientists are not certain exactly why or how migration evolved, although there are some logical theories around. But no matter what the origin of migration, scientists and laymen alike generally agree that the autumn passage of migratory birds is one of the great spectacles of nature. Anyone who has witnessed the high skeins of passing Canada geese in fall or heard the drift of their clamor on chill autumn nights cannot help but agree that there is at least some majesty in the act of migration.

Curiously, however, in contrast to the migration of waterfowl, the passage of land birds, which creates such a stir in spring, is an event marked primarily by obscurity. The journey south in fall for small birds seems almost a filtering process rather than a great wave. Gradually, there seem to be fewer catbirds whining in the shrubbery. Some morning you may happen to notice that there are fewer robins on the lawn. Even the sprightly warblers that were so much a part of the spring migration pass through in dull undistinguished plumage. If anything, there are more warblers now than there were in the spring, since the new crop of young is moving south too, but the presence of the tree leaves and the dull plumage keep them well hidden.

The small birds may be obscure in their migrations, but along with the geese there are two other avian events that add to the spectacle of the fall migration. One is the great rivers of blackbirds that jockey across the evening sky from late August to November. Red-winged blackbirds, grackles, and cowbirds fly south by fits and starts, sometimes moving east and west or even north in their daily passage between feeding and roosting areas. But in spite of the fact that huge flocks may seem to remain in one area for weeks at a time, the general drift is south, and by December they will be gone.

The other observable spectacle of autumn migration is a smaller more intimate event. One of the reasons that passerine birds are rarely seen in the actual act of migration is that many of them migrate at night. Therefore, it is generally difficult to observe the birds, but there are two times during the season when you can witness the night migration. Toward the end of September and again in October on some clear night when the moon is full take a chair out to some good vantage point and focus a telescope or a pair of binoculars on the moon. As you watch, you may notice from time to time the quick, dark forms of migratory birds flit past in silhouette. If the night is still, listen carefully and you will hear the high twitter of obscured flocks and individuals passing overhead. It is an impressive, although intimate, event, and it is typical of the quiet rituals that periodically occur in the natural world and go unnoticed by the average citizen. Certainly the event rivals television for entertainment, and even if you don't happen to see any moon-crossers you will at least be afforded a good view of the autumn moon.

There is one other migratory spectacle that occurs in certain select areas. Throughout the season, from September through November, hawks from the entire northern half of the continent funnel down along mountain ridges to their southern wintering grounds. If you put yourself in the proper place at the proper time, you may be able to witness more hawks in a single day than you will see during the whole course of a year. It is not uncommon, for example, to see two to three thousand broadwings on a good day in the right place, or three to four hundred sharp-shinned hawks. The most famous place in the United States for hawk watching is Hawk Mountain in the Kittatinny mountains in eastern Pennsylvania, but any ridge on a clear warm day with northwest winds in September or October should reveal at least a few migrants.

While you are watching the skies for hawks, you may catch sight of another winged form—the green darner dragonfly. The fact is, birds are not the only creatures that use the air for a migratory route. The green darner and also the monarch butterfly tend to follow the same ridges as the hawks, and generally for the same reasons—they are taking advantage of the updrafts and thermals that occur along mountain ridges. But unlike the hawks, the small weak-winged migratory insects are much more at the mercy of the elements. As a result, you don't have to go to the nearest mountain range to witness their passage. Simply watch the backyard and fields during late September and early October, and you may notice what seems to be a larger than normal number of monarchs and dragonflies. Like the migration of the fall warblers, the passage of the insects is relatively obscured. In fact, although it too involves millions of individuals, for the most part migration goes by unobserved each year except by a choice few.

The green darner and the monarch are unique in the insect world. Generally, insects take a simple although rather extreme solution to the problem of winter; they simply give up and die, leaving behind a great storehouse of eggs and pupae to repopulate once the warm weather returns. Like many of the momentous events that occur in the natural world in fall, the massive death of the vast insect population goes unnoticed. The only real manifestation of the departure is the slow demise of the backyard chorus of insects. By early September the noise of the night-calling insects that began the month before has reached full force. Nightly the unified throbbing of the snowy tree crickets is pierced by the strident rhythms of the katydids and the long-horned grasshoppers. But slowly, night by night as the season moves on, the throb of the snowy tree crickets becomes slower and slower and thinner and thinner until sometime in mid-October it ceases altogether. The small tinkling of the meadow crickets will go on for a few weeks more. In some years on warm nights their bell-like calls may be heard as late as December. But the switches have been thrown—the huge energies of the insect world have been broken by the cold, and life in the woods and fields is stilling down.

Like the day, the year has a way of going out in fire. Whatever splendor may occur in the grass as a result of the dying chorus of the insects is rivaled by the slow, colorful fading that takes place in the plant world. The brilliance of the autumn hills is by far the best-known fall spectacle, but in a smaller way, the products of the summer's growing season provide an equal show in the forms of fruits, nuts, and berries. The wild flowers that brightened the spare light of the spring woods now once more offer a show of color in the rich purples of the Canada mayflowers, the exotic eyelike berry of the baneberry, and the drooping sprays of Solomon's seal. Fat clusters of wild grapes hang from the vines, and the branches of the wild fruit trees, such as the crab apple and the wild plum, provide a rich fare for any number of mammals, including such varied species as deer and foxes and raccoons.

Almost daily the landscape changes as the year grinds towards late fall, and with the dropping of the leaves the world enters into a rust-colored barren season. Late October and early November seem closer to winter than to autumn, but in spite of the apparent stillness, life abounds in the woods and fields. Late November seems to stir a frantic spurt of storage behavior among squirrels, chipmunks, and mice. It is now, on the first chill nights, that the white-footed mouse, in its inestimable wisdom, sees fit to move into the walls of country houses for the winter. And it is now that the chipmunks stock food chambers deep in their tunnels in preparation for the long season underground. The woodchuck grows drowsier and drowsier, emerges less and less from his burrow, and finally ceases to appear. Skunks and the adventurous June litters of raccoons become more and more noticeable as they increase their foraging in an attempt to fatten themselves on the bounty of summer.

But the long feast is almost over. The great engine of the season that began warming itself up sometime in late February is slowly shutting itself off, and by late December, just before the winter solstice, there is a genuine stillness afield that has not existed since the empty days of mid-January. Migratory birds are gone, yet to be replaced by the northern visitors. The woodchucks and the chipmunks have disappeared from the landscape, the meadow crickets are silenced in the frozen grass, and except for a few late-blooming dandelions, the fruits and flowers have withered in the fields. The three-star belt of Orion rises earlier and earlier in the night sky, and even the sun, the very fuel of the seasons, seems to lose its energy as it sweeps lower and lower across the southern horizon.

The Fall Sky

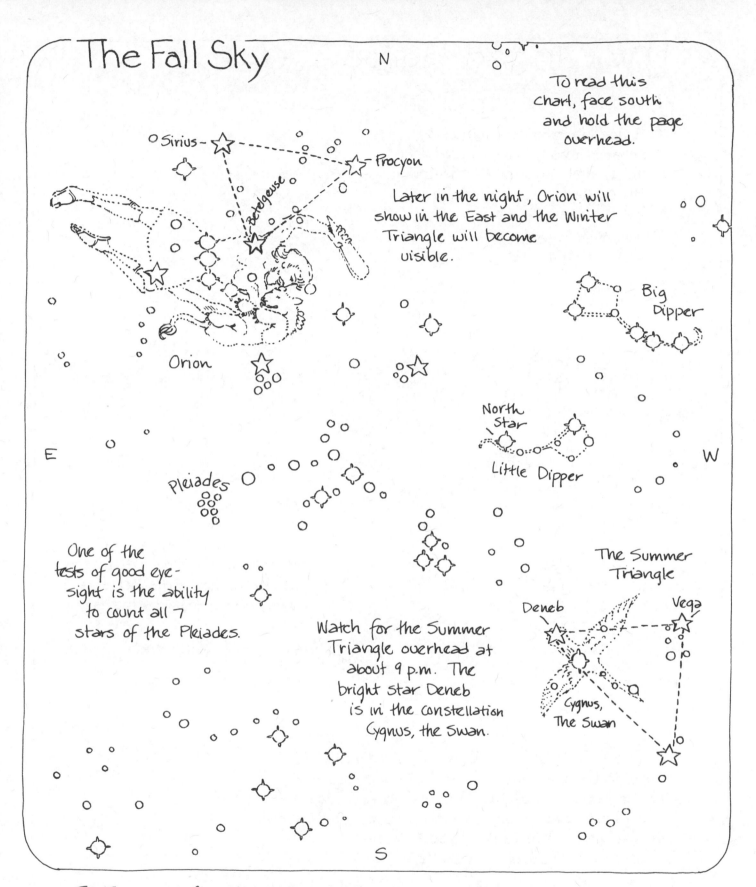

To read this chart, face south and hold the page overhead.

Sirius

Procyon

Betelgeuse

Later in the night, Orion will show in the East and the Winter Triangle will become visible.

Big Dipper

Orion

North Star

Little Dipper

E

W

Pleiades

One of the tests of good eye-sight is the ability to count all 7 stars of the Pleiades.

Watch for the Summer Triangle overhead at about 9 p.m. The bright star Deneb is in the constellation Cygnus, the Swan.

The Summer Triangle

Deneb

Vega

Cygnus, The Swan

S

For Further Information: <u>Stars</u>, Herbert S. Zim and Robert H. Baker, Golden Nature Guide.

The Winged Horse

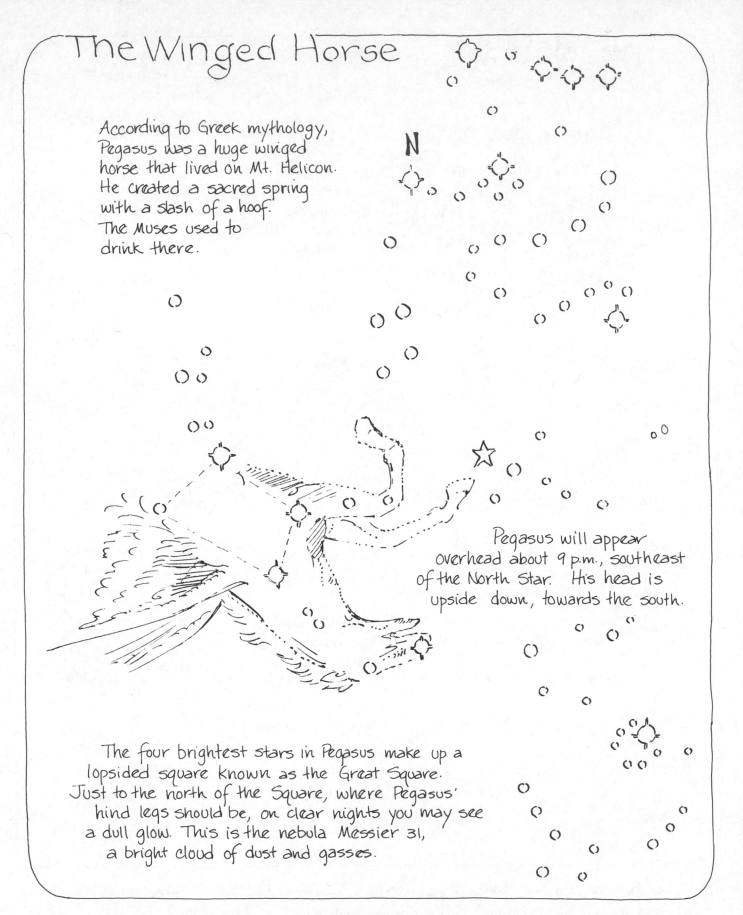

According to Greek mythology,
Pegasus was a huge winged
horse that lived on Mt. Helicon.
He created a sacred spring
with a slash of a hoof.
The Muses used to
drink there.

Pegasus will appear
overhead about 9 p.m., southeast
of the North Star. His head is
upside down, towards the south.

The four brightest stars in Pegasus make up a
lopsided square known as the Great Square.
Just to the north of the Square, where Pegasus'
hind legs should be, on clear nights you may see
a dull glow. This is the nebula Messier 31,
a bright cloud of dust and gasses.

For Further Information: <u>Field Book of the Skies</u>, William T. Olcott, Putnam.

HAWK migration

Red-tailed hawks are the last to go. Peak of their migration is usually in November. Watch for the glint of the red tail as the hawk soars past. Somewhat larger than the stubby broad-winged hawk.

Unlike smaller migratory birds, hawks and eagles take the easy road south, drifting down the drafts of warm air that rise from valley floors in mountainous areas. Watch for them on mountain tops on clear, warm days. Different species migrate at different times during the season. Hawkwatching has developed into a favorite autumn pastime for serious birders. The good watching sites are often crowded.

Broad-winged hawks are the first to leave. Watch for them during the second or third week of September. Look for the banded tail.

Sharp-shinned hawks can be seen in late September or early October.

Ospreys migrate at the same time as the sharp-shinneds. Can be identified by long wings with black spots at the crook.

For Further Information: Watching Birds, An Introduction to Ornithology, Roger F. Pasquier, Houghton Mifflin.

Hawk and Owl Pellets

Hawks and owls regurgitate indigestible material such as fur and feathers in small grayish pellets. You can often find these pellets in the woods where the birds have roosted for the night, or under nest sites.

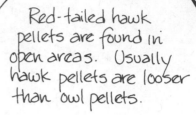

Red-tailed hawk pellets are found in open areas. Usually hawk pellets are looser than owl pellets.

Screech owl pellets are smaller. Often contain feathers.

You can dissect hawk and owl pellets. Soak the pellet in warm water with detergent for an hour or so and then pick it apart with tweezers and needles. The job is easier if it is done on blotting paper.

Look for the great horned owl pellets under conifers in deep woods.

For Further Information: <u>Owls: Their Natural and Unnatural History</u>, John Sparks & Tony Soper, Taplinger Publishing Co.

Mammal Skulls in Pellets

Pellets of hawks and owls furnish clues for determining the diet of predatory birds. The easiest parts to identify are the skulls of small mammals.

Exploded view of a pellet: Look for feathers, bones, complete skulls and teeth. Bird bones are hollow. Note: Fox droppings resemble pellets but are pointed on the ends.

skull

bones

vertebrae

feather

hair

bill

Meadow voles are one of the most commonly eaten mammals. Skull is one inch long.

Deer mouse skull is about one inch. Slightly more squat in appearance than the meadow vole skull.

Short-tail shrew skull is about 3/4 inch. Teeth are tipped with red.

NOTE: SKULL DRAWINGS ARE NOT TO SCALE.

For Further Information: A Field Guide to the Mammals, W.H. Burt and R.P. Grossenheider, Houghton Mifflin.

GEESE IN PASSAGE

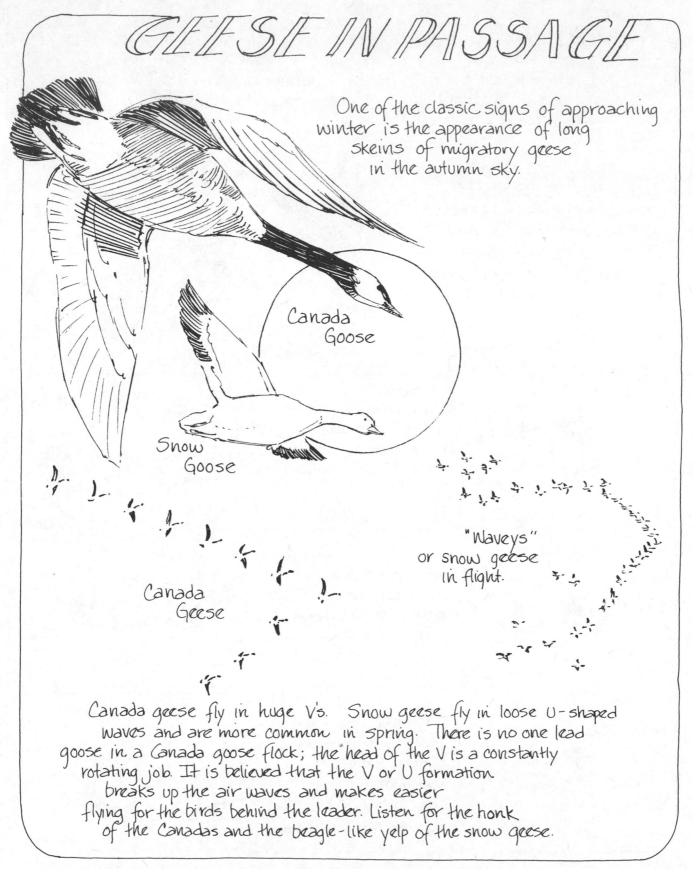

One of the classic signs of approaching winter is the appearance of long skeins of migratory geese in the autumn sky.

Canada Goose

Snow Goose

"Waveys" or snow geese in flight.

Canada Geese

Canada geese fly in huge V's. Snow geese fly in loose U-shaped waves and are more common in spring. There is no one lead goose in a Canada goose flock; the head of the V is a constantly rotating job. It is believed that the V or U formation breaks up the air waves and makes easier flying for the birds behind the leader. Listen for the honk of the Canadas and the beagle-like yelp of the snow geese.

For Further Information: _The Ducks, Geese and Swans of North America_, Francis H. Kortright, The Stackpole Co.

A guide to winter finches

One of the little-known signs of the coming winter is the arrival of the so-called winter finches. These birds spend the summer in the northern forest. In late fall, every other year, they come south in large flights for the winter season. Watch for them at your bird feeder.

Purple finches can be found throughout the year, but they are more obvious in winter. Males are a rosy-red color. As spring approaches, listen to their long, rollicking song.

The evening grosbeak is perhaps the most common winter finch. They are hogs for sun-flower seed. Sometimes occur in huge flocks.

Pine grosbeaks are the same color as purple finches, but they have fat beaks. The males have white wing-bars. Pine grosbeaks, redpolls and other winter finches do not appear every year.

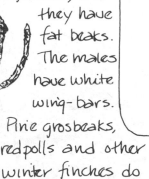

Look for the pine siskin in flocks in tree-tops. Except for the thin bill, they look like active sparrows. Fond of red cedar.

Redpolls look like pink-breasted sparrows with a black chin. They often come to feeders. Like the other winter finches, they are abundant only in certain years.

For Further Information: <u>Birds of North America</u>, Chandler Robbins, Golden Press.

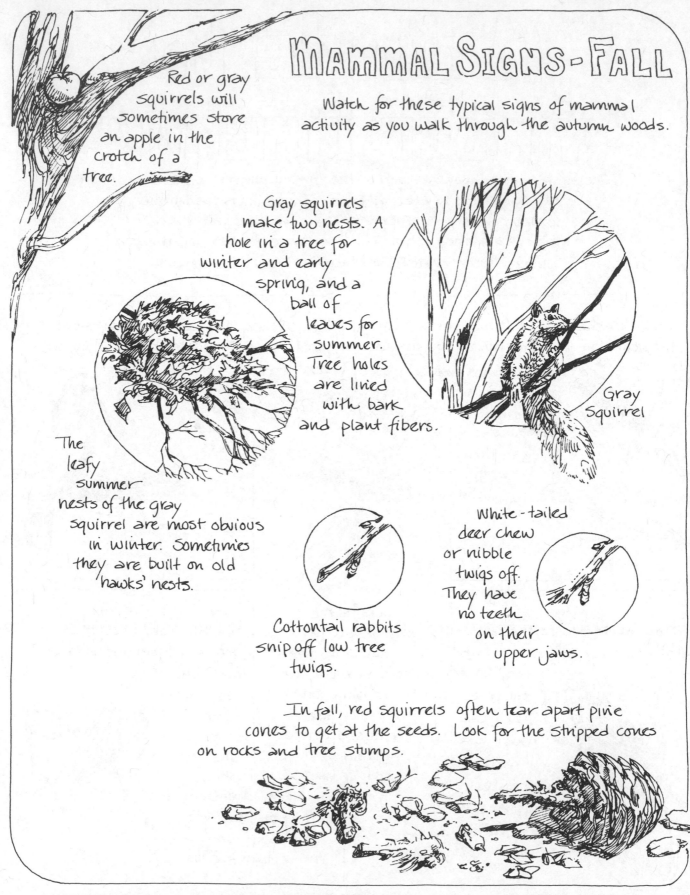

Mammal Signs - Fall

Watch for these typical signs of mammal activity as you walk through the autumn woods.

Red or gray squirrels will sometimes store an apple in the crotch of a tree.

Gray squirrels make two nests. A hole in a tree for winter and early spring, and a ball of leaves for summer. Tree holes are lined with bark and plant fibers.

Gray Squirrel

The leafy summer nests of the gray squirrel are most obvious in winter. Sometimes they are built on old hawks' nests.

Cottontail rabbits snip off low tree twigs.

White-tailed deer chew or nibble twigs off. They have no teeth on their upper jaws.

In fall, red squirrels often tear apart pine cones to get at the seeds. Look for the stripped cones on rocks and tree stumps.

For Further Information: A Field Guide to Animal Tracks, Olaus Murie, Houghton Mifflin.

MAMMALS UNDERGROUND

With the coming of fall, ground-dwelling mammals begin to prepare for winter. The woodchuck fattens itself for hibernation. Chipmunks begin to stock their underground storage chambers and moles retreat to deeper tunnels below the frost line. For all but the hibernating woodchuck, life goes on during the winter months. Chipmunks sleep more, but they wake periodically to feed.

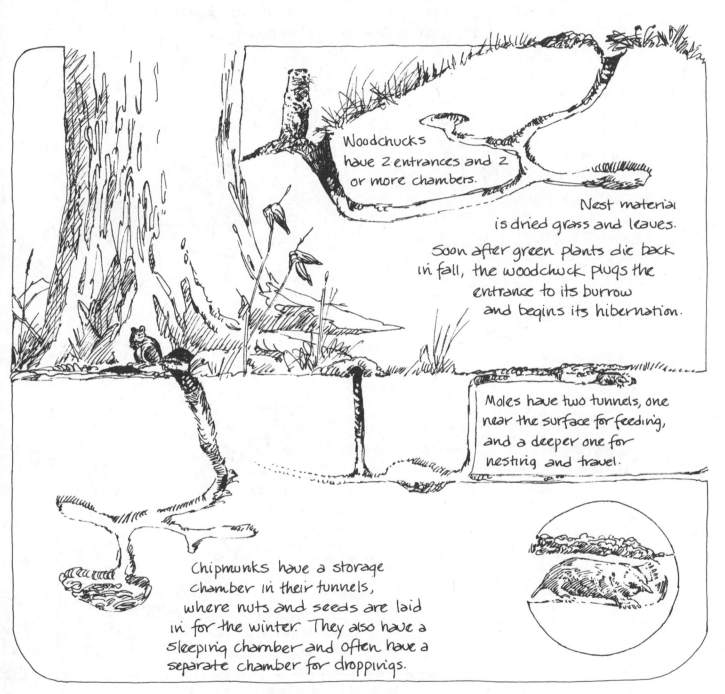

Woodchucks have 2 entrances and 2 or more chambers.

Nest material is dried grass and leaves.

Soon after green plants die back in fall, the woodchuck plugs the entrance to its burrow and begins its hibernation.

Moles have two tunnels, one near the surface for feeding, and a deeper one for nesting and travel.

Chipmunks have a storage chamber in their tunnels, where nuts and seeds are laid in for the winter. They also have a sleeping chamber and often have a separate chamber for droppings.

For Further Information: <u>A Field Guide to the Mammals</u>, W. H. Burt and R. P. Gossenheider, Houghton Mifflin.

HOW WASPS AND BEES SPEND THE WINTER

Surviving the freezing temperatures of winter is a major problem for creatures like insects which do not produce their own body heat. Wasps and bees have developed several different methods of solving this problem.

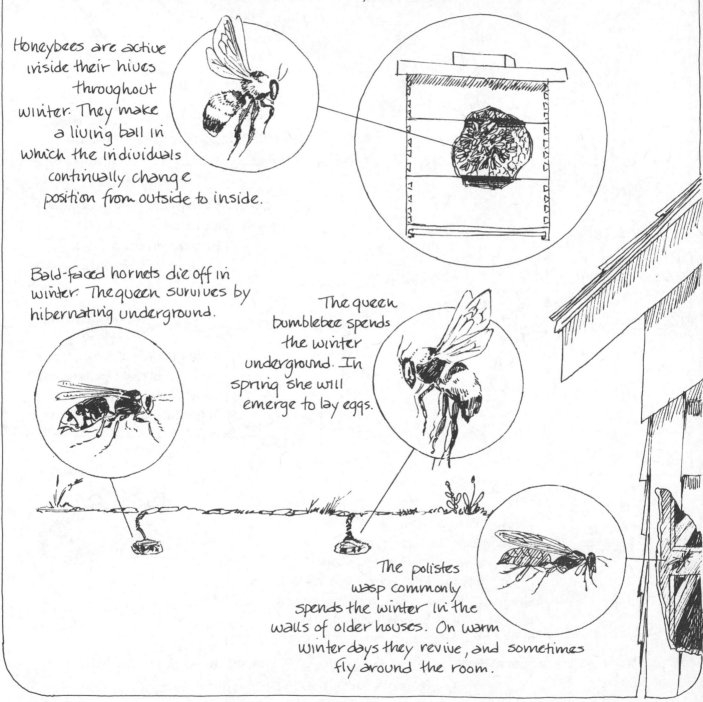

Honeybees are active inside their hives throughout winter. They make a living ball in which the individuals continually change position from outside to inside.

Bald-faced hornets die off in winter. The queen survives by hibernating underground.

The queen bumblebee spends the winter underground. In spring she will emerge to lay eggs.

The polistes wasp commonly spends the winter in the walls of older houses. On warm winter days they revive, and sometimes fly around the room.

For Further Information: <u>Man and Insects</u>, L. H. Newman, Natural History Press.

DRAGONFLY migration

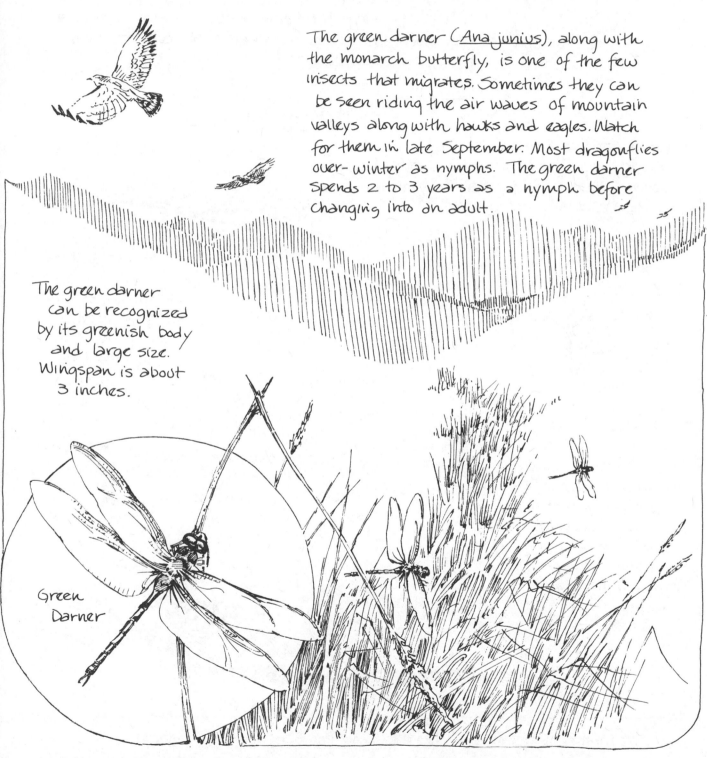

The green darner (_Ana junius_), along with the monarch butterfly, is one of the few insects that migrates. Sometimes they can be seen riding the air waves of mountain valleys along with hawks and eagles. Watch for them in late September. Most dragonflies over-winter as nymphs. The green darner spends 2 to 3 years as a nymph before changing into an adult.

The green darner can be recognized by its greenish body and large size. Wingspan is about 3 inches.

Green Darner

For Further Information : <u>Field Book of Insects</u>, Frank E. Lutz, Putnam.

SLUGS AND SNAILS

Slugs and snails belong to the group of animals known as the mollusks, a group that includes clams, oysters, whelks, and other shelled creatures. Snails have full shells; slugs have only a thin plate or no shell at all. Many species are scavengers, although they can also be a pest in gardens.

Watch for slug trails on blacktopped roads in early morning. Slugs and snails lay down a bed of mucus as they move. They are mostly nocturnal.

Gray Field Slug:
Can be a pest in gardens. A pan of beer or a bed of fine ashes will help control them. Shell is a thin plate.

Land Snail:
Watch for the spire-like shell. Commonly found in upland areas. Can be a garden pest in wet seasons. Land snails lay eggs in May or October. Some individuals winter over as adults.

White-lipped Land Snail:
Look for the white border on the opening of the shell.
A favorite food of shrews.

For Further Information: How to Know the Eastern Land Snails, John B. Burch, Wm. C. Brown Co.

THE FALL CANKERWORM

Fall cankerworms feed on the fruit and leaves of apple and pear trees as well as ornamental trees. They belong to a family known as the geometrid moths. Adults fly mainly at night and are attracted to lights. Watch for them on warm fall evenings.

Female moths are wingless and plump. Larvae burrow underground in early summer and emerge in autumn. Sometimes they winter over until spring.

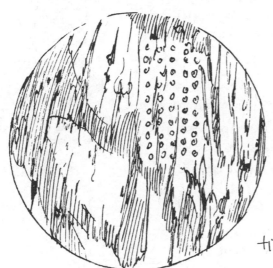

Eggs are laid on deciduous trees in November. Look like tiny flowerpots.

The larva of the fall cankerworm is commonly referred to as the inch worm. They appear in June. Folklore has it that if you find an inch worm on your clothes, you will soon get new clothing.

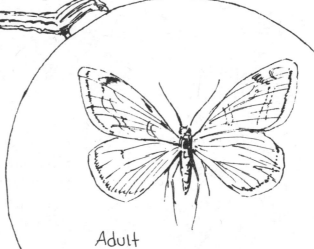

Adult males are gray to brown with two white stripes on the forewing.

For Further Information: <u>Field Book of Insects</u>, Frank E. Lutz, Putnam.

a guide to nuts

In the old days, one of the common pastimes of fall was nut-gathering. Teams of children would go into the woods with sticks to knock down chestnuts, hickories and walnuts before the squirrels could get them. Nutting is a pastime which deserves to be restored. In good years a full supply of nuts can be gathered in a short time.

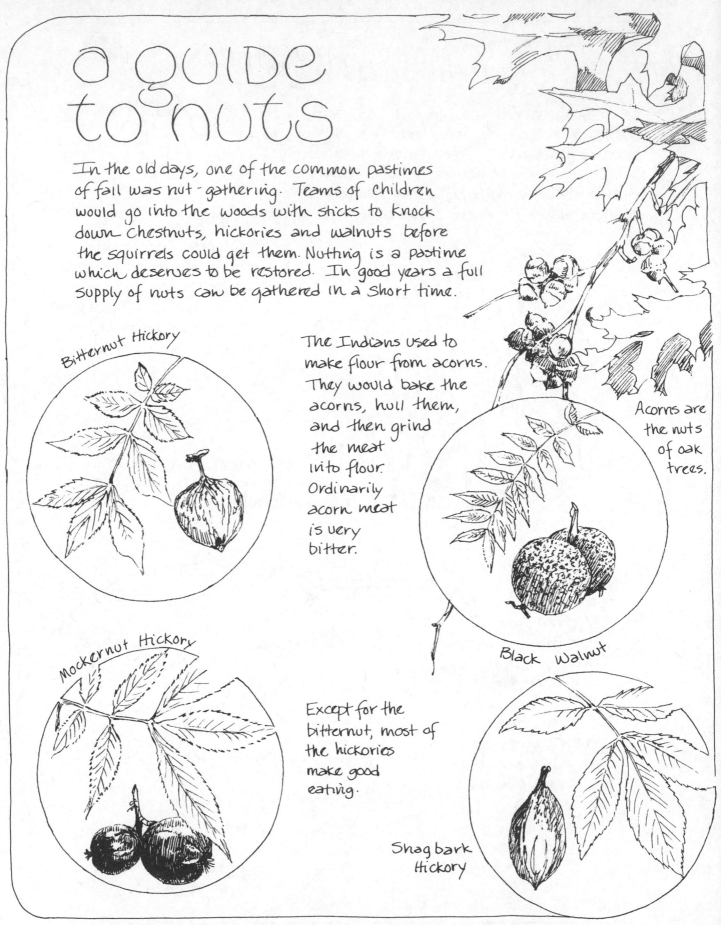

The Indians used to make flour from acorns. They would bake the acorns, hull them, and then grind the meat into flour. Ordinarily acorn meat is very bitter.

Acorns are the nuts of oak trees.

Bitternut Hickory

Black Walnut

Mockernut Hickory

Except for the bitternut, most of the hickories make good eating.

Shagbark Hickory

For Further Information: The Tree Identification Book, George W. D. Symonds, William Morrow & Company.

GOLDENRODS & ASTERS

GOLDENRODS

There are about 65 different species of goldenrods in the United States. They grow in 5 basic shapes. Learn the shapes first, you can learn the species later.

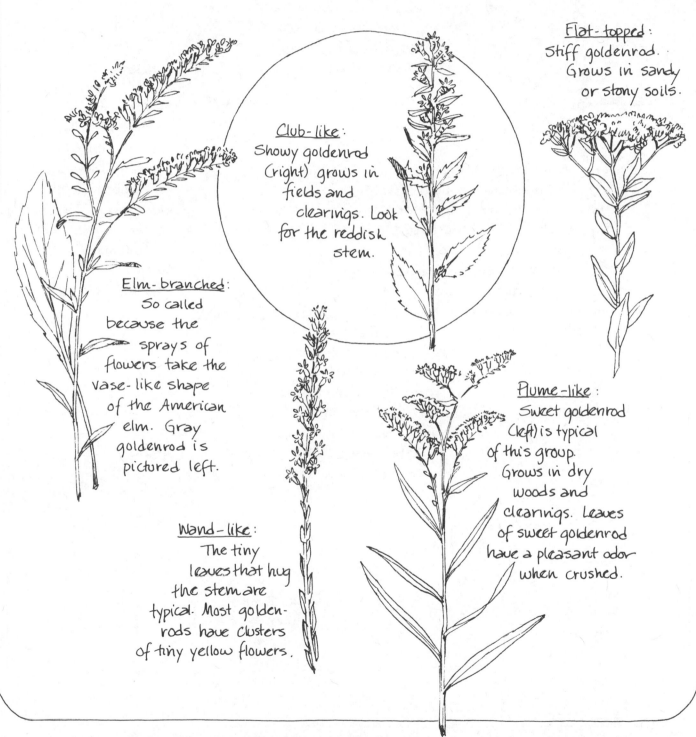

Flat-topped: Stiff goldenrod. Grows in sandy or stony soils.

Club-like: Showy goldenrod (right) grows in fields and clearings. Look for the reddish stem.

Elm-branched: So called because the sprays of flowers take the vase-like shape of the American elm. Gray goldenrod is pictured left.

Plume-like: Sweet goldenrod (left) is typical of this group. Grows in dry woods and clearings. Leaves of sweet goldenrod have a pleasant odor when crushed.

Wand-like: The tiny leaves that hug the stem are typical. Most goldenrods have clusters of tiny yellow flowers.

For Further Information: <u>Newcomb's Wildflower Guide</u>, Laurence Newcomb, Little, Brown and Company.

ASTERS

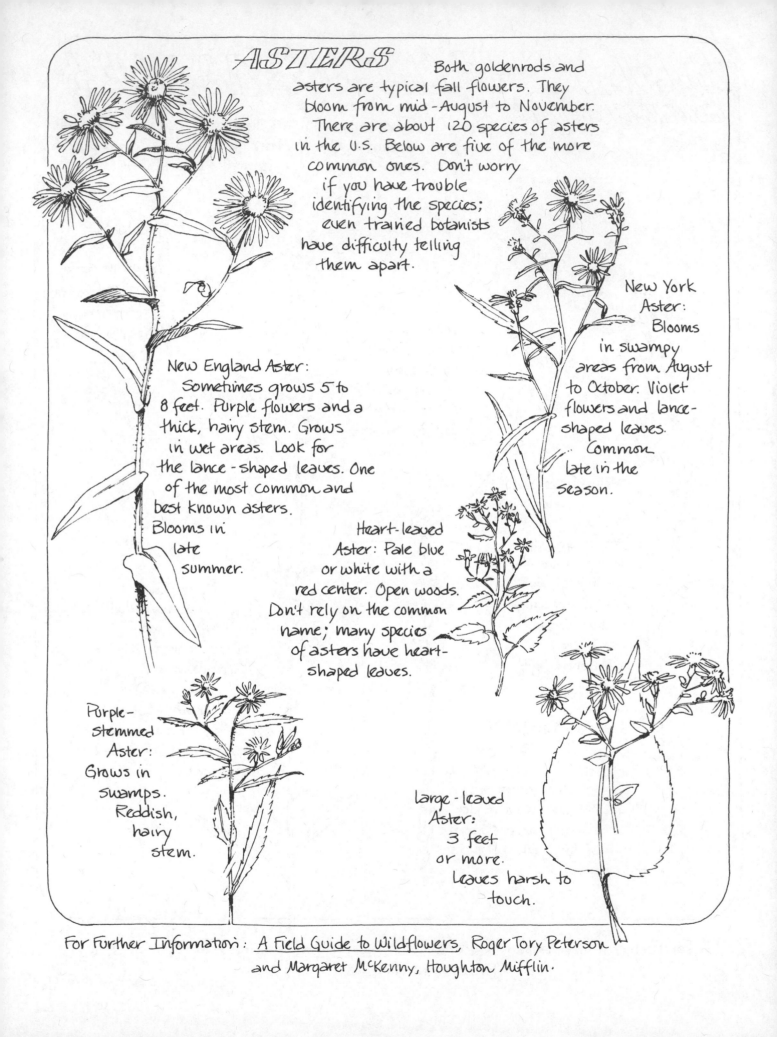

Both goldenrods and asters are typical fall flowers. They bloom from mid-August to November. There are about 120 species of asters in the U.S. Below are five of the more common ones. Don't worry if you have trouble identifying the species; even trained botanists have difficulty telling them apart.

New York Aster: Blooms in swampy areas from August to October. Violet flowers and lance-shaped leaves. Common late in the season.

New England Aster: Sometimes grows 5 to 8 feet. Purple flowers and a thick, hairy stem. Grows in wet areas. Look for the lance-shaped leaves. One of the most common and best known asters. Blooms in late summer.

Heart-leaved Aster: Pale blue or white with a red center. Open woods. Don't rely on the common name; many species of asters have heart-shaped leaves.

Purple-stemmed Aster: Grows in swamps. Reddish, hairy stem.

Large-leaved Aster: 3 feet or more. Leaves harsh to touch.

For Further Information: <u>A Field Guide to Wildflowers,</u> Roger Tory Peterson and Margaret McKenny, Houghton Mifflin.

LEAVES WITHOUT TEETH

Most tree leaves have teeth of one size or another. Here are some of the few leaves with no teeth. Bear in mind that the species pictured are in no way related to each other. The trees come from a variety of families.

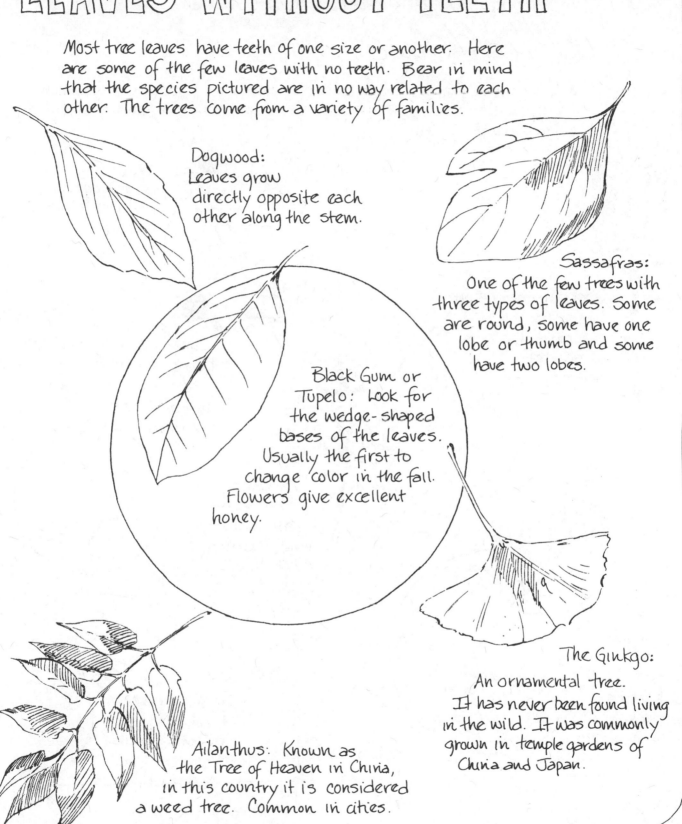

Dogwood: Leaves grow directly opposite each other along the stem.

Sassafras: One of the few trees with three types of leaves. Some are round, some have one lobe or thumb and some have two lobes.

Black Gum or Tupelo: Look for the wedge-shaped bases of the leaves. Usually the first to change color in the fall. Flowers give excellent honey.

The Ginkgo: An ornamental tree. It has never been found living in the wild. It was commonly grown in temple gardens of China and Japan.

Ailanthus: Known as the Tree of Heaven in China, in this country it is considered a weed tree. Common in cities.

For Further Information: <u>Master Tree Finder</u>, May Theilgaard Watts, Nature Study Guide.

Fruits of the Woodland Wildflowers

Woodland wildflowers offer a double reward to those who learn them. They provide beautiful flowers in spring and summer and brightly colored fruits in fall.

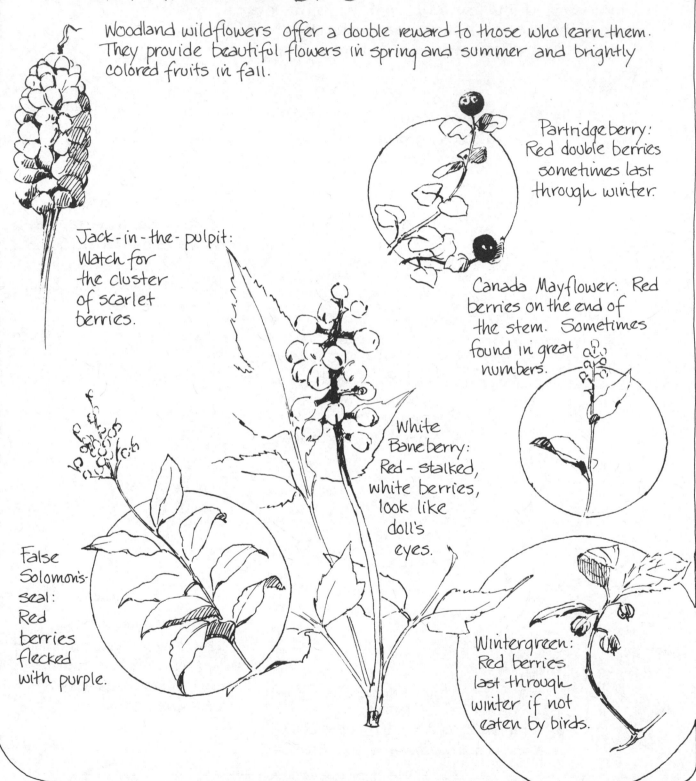

Partridgeberry: Red double berries sometimes last through winter.

Jack-in-the-pulpit: Watch for the cluster of scarlet berries.

Canada Mayflower: Red berries on the end of the stem. Sometimes found in great numbers.

White Baneberry: Red-stalked, white berries, look like doll's eyes.

False Solomon's-seal: Red berries flecked with purple.

Wintergreen: Red berries last through winter if not eaten by birds.

For Further Information: <u>How to Know the Wildflowers</u>, Mrs. William S. Dana, Dover Publications.

Vines in fall

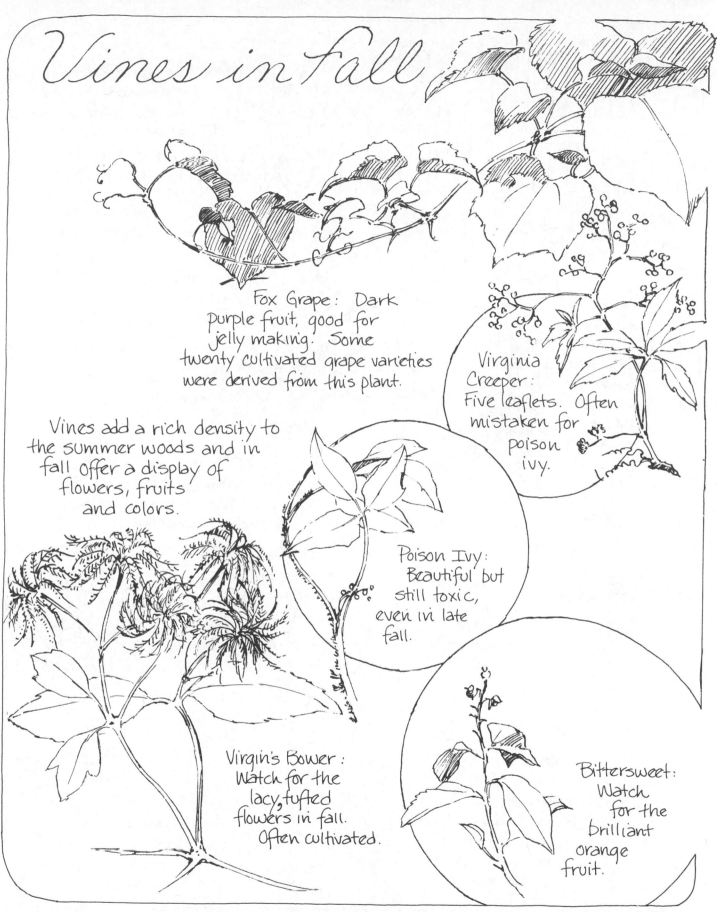

Fox Grape: Dark purple fruit, good for jelly making. Some twenty cultivated grape varieties were derived from this plant.

Virginia Creeper: Five leaflets. Often mistaken for poison ivy.

Vines add a rich density to the summer woods and in fall offer a display of flowers, fruits and colors.

Poison Ivy: Beautiful but still toxic, even in late fall.

Virgin's Bower: Watch for the lacy, tufted flowers in fall. Often cultivated.

Bittersweet: Watch for the brilliant orange fruit.

For Further Information: <u>A Field Guide to Trees and Shrubs</u>, George A. Petrides, Houghton Mifflin Co.

GATHER your own Bird Food

The plants we refer to as weeds provide an abundance of food for birds in winter. Try gathering some to attract birds to your feeder. Below are some of the more favored plants.

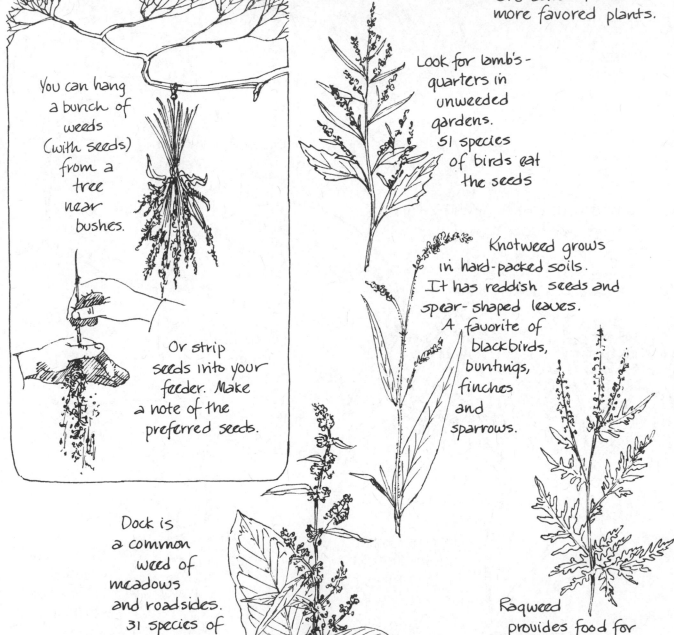

You can hang a bunch of weeds (with seeds) from a tree near bushes.

Or strip seeds into your feeder. Make a note of the preferred seeds.

Look for lamb's-quarters in unweeded gardens. 51 species of birds eat the seeds

Knotweed grows in hard-packed soils. It has reddish seeds and spear-shaped leaves. A favorite of blackbirds, buntings, finches and sparrows.

Dock is a common weed of meadows and roadsides. 31 species of birds eat the seeds.

Ragweed provides food for some 64 species of birds.

For Further Information: <u>Common Weeds of the United States,</u> U.S. Department of Agriculture, Dover.

HITCHHIKERS

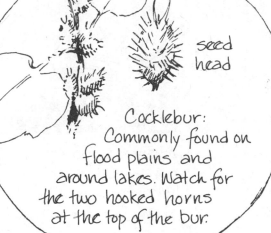

Seeds have a number of ways of spreading themselves around. Some are blown by the wind, some are eaten and digested by birds and mammals and some are equipped with stickers and are carried from place to place on fur or clothing.

seed head

Cocklebur: Commonly found on flood plains and around lakes. Watch for the two hooked horns at the top of the bur.

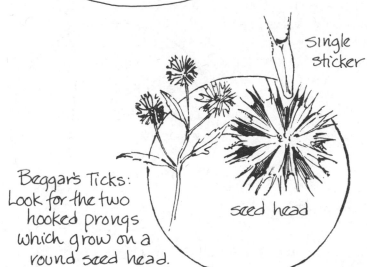

single sticker

seed head

Beggar's Ticks: Look for the two hooked prongs which grow on a round seed head.

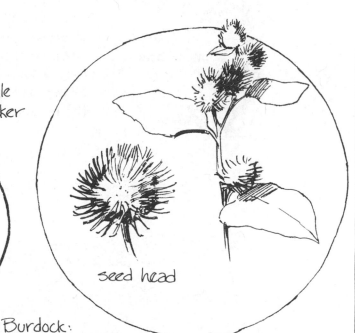

seed head

Burdock: Perhaps the most common and obvious of the hitchhikers. Burs often become hopelessly entangled in the fur of long-haired dogs.

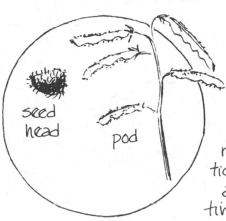

seed head

pod

Tick Trefoil: Sometimes referred to as beggar's ticks. The tiny pods are covered with tiny hooked hairs.

For Further Information: <u>Seeds by Wind and Water</u>, Helene J. Jordan, Crowell.

Common Gilled Mushrooms

Many of the common mushrooms you will find in fall have thin strips of flesh under their caps known as gills. The color and shape of the gills is an important key for mushroom identification.

Mushroom spores are formed inside the gills. Wherever a spore lands a new mushroom will grow if the conditions are favorable.

Meadow Mushroom

Mushrooms are like the flower or fruiting body of the group of non-flowering plants known as the fungi. The other part of the plant is a thread-like mass of material known as the mycelium.

Fairy Ring.

Look for the rings of mushrooms after rains.

Cap

Gills

Veil

Volva

Chanterelle has fat, thickened gills which run down the stem.

The Destroying Angel (Amanita virosa) is the most toxic mushroom known. Usually pure white with a skirt-like veil and a bulb, or volva, at the base of the stem. It is so deadly some people wash their hands after handling it.

Shaggy Mane has its gills hidden beneath its long cap.

For Further Information: <u>Mushroom Hunter's Field Guide</u>, Alexander Smith, Charles Scribner's Sons.

backyard sanctuary
PLANT A SPRUCE

A spruce tree planted in the path of the prevailing winter winds will provide shelter and cover for visitors at the bird feeder. During spring it will offer nesting sites for birds such as the purple finch or mourning dove, and pine siskins and pine grosbeaks will feed on the fruits in early winter.

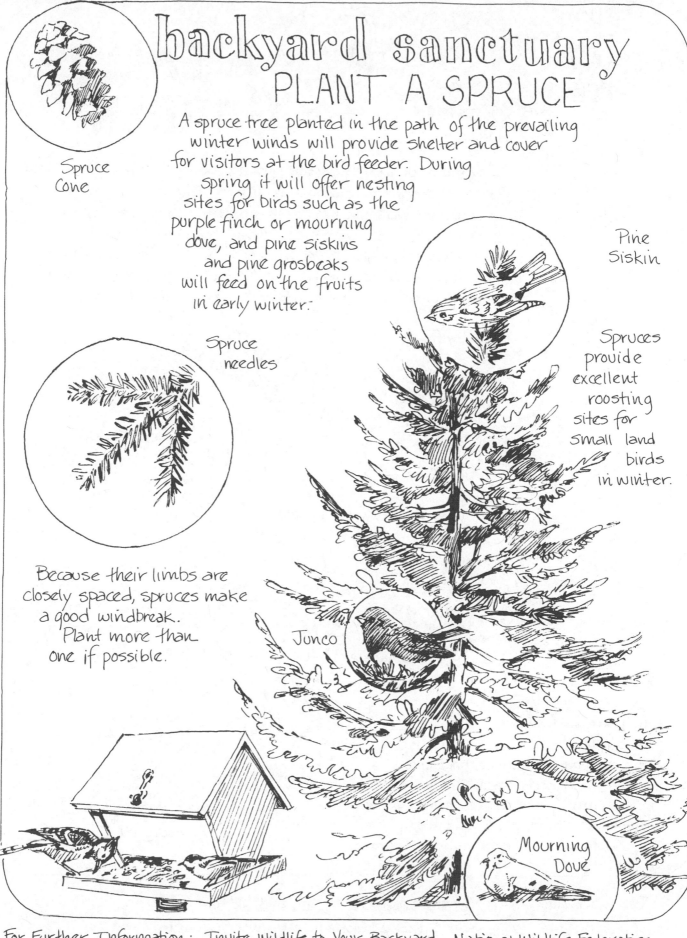

Spruce Cone

Pine Siskin

Spruce needles

Spruces provide excellent roosting sites for small land birds in winter.

Because their limbs are closely spaced, spruces make a good windbreak. Plant more than one if possible.

Junco

Mourning Dove

For Further Information: _Invite Wildlife to Your Backyard_, National Wildlife Federation.

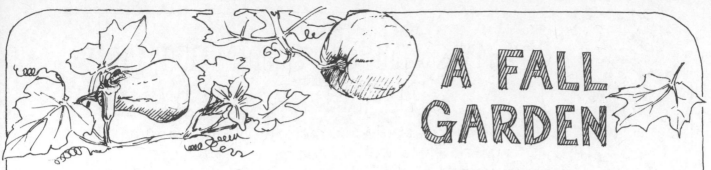

A FALL GARDEN

Don't give up on the garden just because the first light frost has blackened a few squash plants. There are a lot of vegetables that can be grown up until the first snows. Collards, kale and mustard all can stand frost, and you can even get a head start on spring by planting carrots now. Be sure all these plants are well protected with mulch, or cover them with old storm windows to form a small greenhouse.

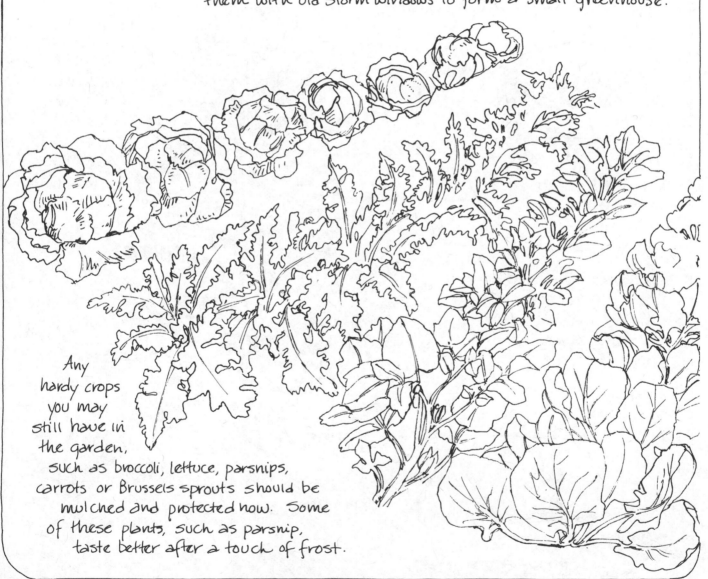

Any hardy crops you may still have in the garden, such as broccoli, lettuce, parsnips, carrots or Brussels sprouts should be mulched and protected now. Some of these plants, such as parsnip, taste better after a touch of frost.

For Further Information: _Growing Up Green – Parents and Children Gardening,_ Alice S. Kelsey & Gloria Huckaby, Workman Pub. Co.

FALL CARE OF THE GARDEN...
PLANT A COVER CROP

Growing vegetables takes nutrients out of the soil. You can replace nutrients by planting a cover crop in the fall. The crops not only protect the soil during winter, they add structure to the soil after they are turned under in the spring.

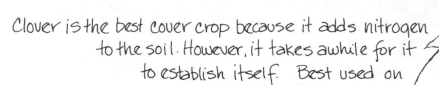

Clover is the best cover crop because it adds nitrogen to the soil. However, it takes awhile for it to establish itself. Best used on a garden patch that will lie fallow for a season.

Rye is one of the most commonly used cover crops in larger gardens and fields. Will grow even on warm winter days.

Buckwheat grows very quickly, but is subject to frost.

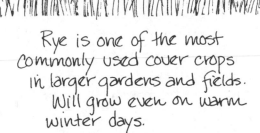

Clean up old garden debris and spread cover crop seed generously, preferably before frost.

Turn under the cover crop in the early spring with a fork or roto-tiller.

For Further Information: <u>The Basic Book of Organic Gardening</u>, Robert Rodale, Rodale Press.

The Folklore of Forecasting

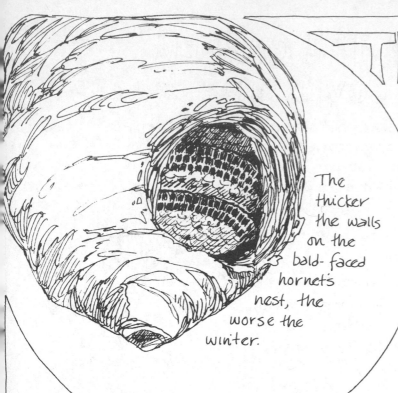

The thicker the walls on the bald-faced hornet's nest, the worse the winter.

Before the age of scientific weather forecasting, farmers and country people used to watch for natural signs to help predict the weather. Much of this weather lore attempted to forecast the harshness of the coming winter.

A wide band on the woolly bear caterpillar means a bad winter.

High beaver and muskrat lodges mean the winter will be harsh.

Although some of the folklore of forecasting is accurate, the methods on these pages are all false. The reasons should be obvious. Animals and plants can't predict the flukes of weather patterns any better than the weathermen.

The larger the crop of acorns, the longer the winter.

For Further Information: <u>Folklore of American Weather</u>, Eric Sloane, Hawthorn. <u>Weather Wisdom</u>, Albert Lee, Doubleday.

apple heads

1 Peel and core a green apple.

2 As the apple dries, mold eyes, nose and mouth.

In rural areas in good harvest years, corn and apples provided the raw material for younger toymakers. Here are a few ideas for old-fashioned playthings.

4 Dry in a warm oven for 10 or 15 minutes.

3 Soak the apple head in salt water for ½ hour to prevent discoloring.

5 Decorate with grass, moss, or the like.

For Further Information: <u>Nature Crafts</u>, Ellsworth Jaeger, Macmillan.

CORN THINGS

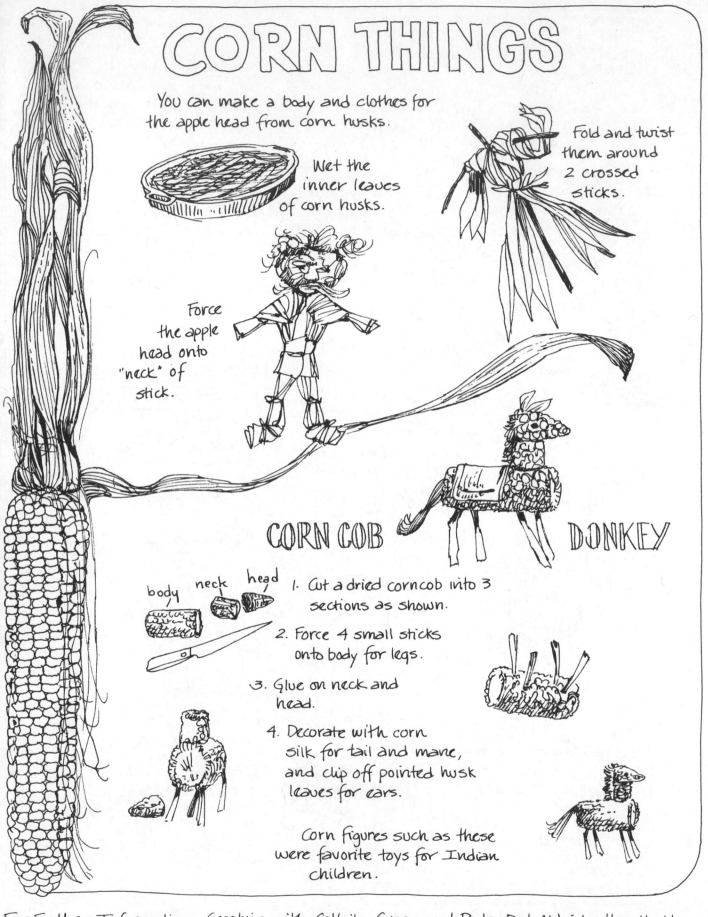

You can make a body and clothes for the apple head from corn husks.

Wet the inner leaves of corn husks.

Fold and twist them around 2 crossed sticks.

Force the apple head onto "neck" of stick.

CORN COB   DONKEY

body   neck   head

1. Cut a dried corncob into 3 sections as shown.

2. Force 4 small sticks onto body for legs.

3. Glue on neck and head.

4. Decorate with corn silk for tail and mane, and clip off pointed husk leaves for ears.

Corn figures such as these were favorite toys for Indian children.

For Further Information: *Creating with Cattails, Cones and Pods*, Dot Aldrich, Hearthside.

BARK RUBBINGS

You can collect the interesting bark patterns of different trees by using the same techniques as gravestone rubbing. Flat-barked trees such as the ones below work the best. Be sure the tree bark you are working with is free of moss and lichens, and be sure to label your rubbing when it is completed. Once you know the bark patterns of different species, you will know the trees in any season.

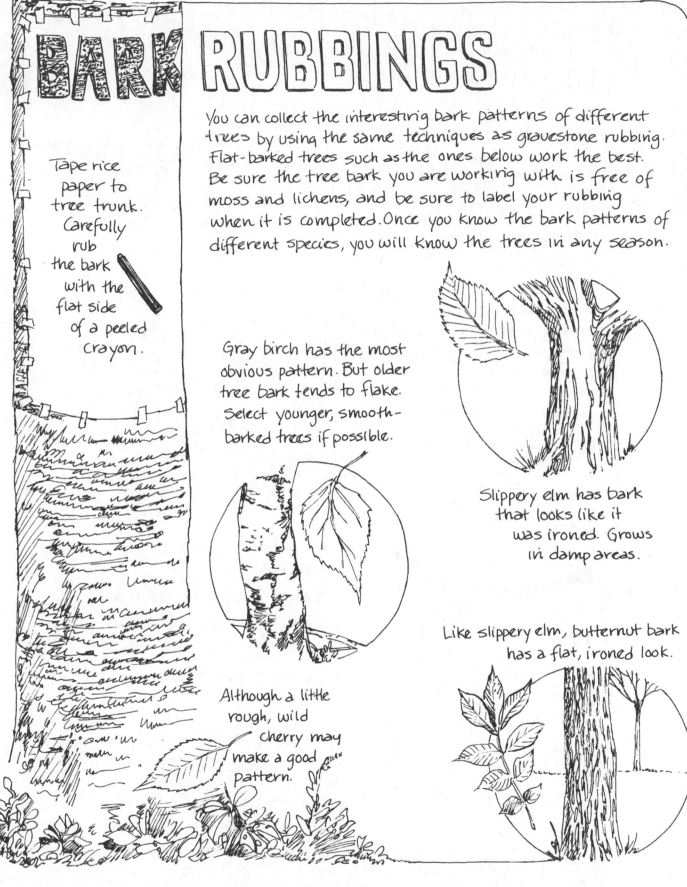

Tape rice paper to tree trunk. Carefully rub the bark with the flat side of a peeled crayon.

Gray birch has the most obvious pattern. But older tree bark tends to flake. Select younger, smooth-barked trees if possible.

Slippery elm has bark that looks like it was ironed. Grows in damp areas.

Like slippery elm, butternut bark has a flat, ironed look.

Although a little rough, wild cherry may make a good pattern.

For Further Information: _Enjoying Nature with Your Family_, Michael Chinery, Crown Publishers.

HowTo
DRY FALL FLOWERS

It is not necessary to go to the florist to buy dried flower arrangements for decoration. You can save a small part of summer by drying your own flowers.

1. Fill bottom of jar with the corn meal mix.

2. Insert the flower upside down.

3. Gently cover the rest of the flower with the corn meal mix.

4. Let sit 10 days to 2 weeks.

Certain cultivated flowers, such as straw flowers, are bred specifically for drying. Be sure to try drying wildflowers as well as garden varieties. They dry just as well, and are considerably cheaper.

Mix: 6 parts white corn meal to 1 part Borax.

For Further Information: *Keeping the Plants You Pick*, Laura Louise Foster, Crowell.

natural dyes...
dye plants for fall

Until the advent of aniline dyes around 1850, most material was colored with dye obtained from plants. Some dye plants were cultivated, but many dyes were obtained from wild plants, especially in this country.

Goldenrod flower heads give a yellow color. Best if picked early.

Burdock leaves can be boiled to obtain a yellow dye.

Butternut hulls will dye material a beautiful tan. It was the standard dye of the pioneers.

Dandelion roots will give a red to violet color. Stems and leaves, a greenish-yellow.

Root bark of sassafras makes a rose-tan dye.

For Further Information: <u>Nature's Colors: Dyes From Plants</u>, Ida Grae, Macmillan Publishing Co.

how to dye material
preparation of the leaves or roots

Best results are obtained if plant material is chopped into fine pieces and soaked overnight.

plant dye ... will take best if material is soaked in a mordant before dyeing begins. To make a mordant for 1/4 pound of wool, mix one ounce of alum in one gallon water. For cotton, add 1/4 ounce of washing soda to the mixture.

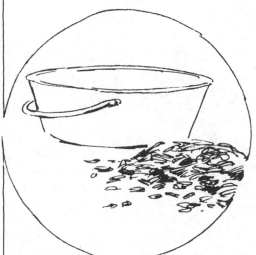

4. Rinse dyed material in hot water and cool gradually until clear. Dry in shade.

1. Simmer the mixture for an hour or so and strain off the liquid.

2. Soak the material in the mordant overnight.

3. Take material from mordant, squeeze out and simmer in water mixed with the dye plant material until the dye takes.

For Further Information: <u>Natural Dyes: Plants and Processes</u>, Jack Kramer, Charles Scribner's Sons.

How to Make Spore Prints

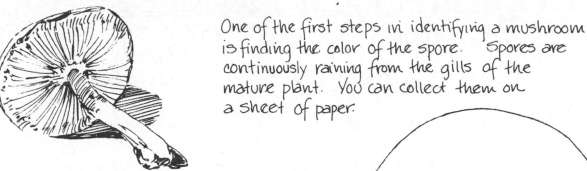

One of the first steps in identifying a mushroom is finding the color of the spore. Spores are continuously raining from the gills of the mature plant. You can collect them on a sheet of paper.

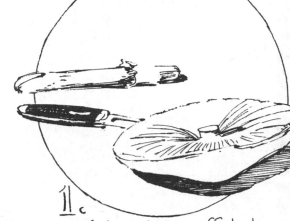

1. Cut mushroom off at stem.

2. To preserve the spores, coat a sheet of construction paper with gum arabic.

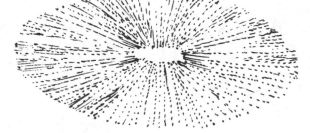

The finished print: some of the spores are beautifully colored, and the designs are always interesting.

3. Place the mushroom face down on the paper. Cover with a bowl and let it sit overnight.

Carefully remove mushroom cap from paper in the morning.

To preserve the spore print, spray it with a fine varnish spray. Be sure to spray very lightly so as not to disturb the spores, and give the print several coats.

For Further Information: Wildcrafts, Leslie Linsey, Doubleday.

A CALENDAR OF NATURAL EVENTS

MONTH	1st week	2nd week	3rd week	4th week
SEPT.				Mushrooms appear after rains. Fall webworm webs. Monarch butterfly migration.
OCT.	Fall fruits. Sharp-shinned hawk migration.	Vine berries appear. Sensitive ferns hit by frosts. Juncos arrive. Fall color at height.	Nuts ripe. Blackbird migration. Yellow-rumped warblers migrate.	Grosbeaks and purple finches arrive. Chipmunks go under-ground.
NOV.	Canada geese migrate. Listen for the last calls of the meadow crickets. Red-tailed hawks migrate.	Fall cankerworms emerge. Slugs and snails go into hibernation. Watch for old birds' nests as leaves go.	Wasps leave paper nests for nooks and crevices. Deer herds gathering. Witch hazel in bloom.	Early snows. Pine grosbeaks arrive. Milkweed pods open.
DEC.	Starling flocks form. Redpolls arrive. Watch for lingering migrants.	Watch for the winter coats of small mammals. Goldfinches active.	Ducks active as ponds freeze over. Watch for wintergreen and partridge berries. Winter solstice.	Watch for new birds at feeders as snows come in. Orion visible.

Winter

One of the enduring terrors for primitive man was the possibility of the sun's disappearance. Each year, as the month of December draws to a close, the days grow shorter, the weak sun rises later and crosses the southern horizon in a low arc to set earlier and earlier in the southwest. In the past, there was no guarantee that the sun would not continue in this course and disappear altogether. In the mind of primitive man it was only the intervention of divinely appointed priests and specialized rituals that insured the sun's return. From Stonehenge in Britain, to the arid canyons of the American southwest, men designed primitive celestial tracking systems to chart the course of the sun and the planets. And throughout the world, the weeks following the winter solstice were traditionally a time for celebration.

We are perhaps somewhat more secure in our time, at least in terms of celestial events, but in the natural world, the weeks and months following the winter solstice are the hardest of the year. Winter is serious business in the woods and fields; ice storms, heavy snows, and high winds sometimes devastate trees and branches in older forests. A hard freeze that reaches the bottom mud of shallow ponds can wipe out a season's crop of hibernating bullfrog tadpoles as well as fish and adult frogs and submerged vegetation. A bitter winter with high winds and no snow cover can kill perennial plants and freeze the woodchucks in their burrows. Fortunately, however, evolution has provided various tools for survival of species as a whole, if not of individuals, and except in cases of climatic change the natural world always seems to pull through.

Ironically, in some ways the best insurance against winter overkill is the very symbol of winter itself—namely, snow. The image of the blanket of snow, trite as it may sound, is not entirely inaccurate. Studies have shown that quite apart from the fact that it literally covers everything, snow also tends to keep the earth at ground level considerably warmer than the "outside" air. What is more, for some species, life beneath this huge benign blanket continues with all the energy of summer. The ubiquitous meadow mole, perhaps the most common mammal in the United States, maintains an elaborate system of runways beneath the snow cover, and within these runways a whole ecology of mammal life carries on. Several species of shrews may use the meadow vole tunnels and occasionally, much to the detriment of the smaller mammals, a short-tailed weasel may find its way into the runways and hunt through the maze for the passing voles and shrews.

But in spite of the activity beneath the blanket, it is the mammal life above the snow that creates the real show of winter, at least for the human community. Snow cover, especially a light snow on a hard crust, lays down a ledger upon which a record of the night's activities are written. Even though several of the more common mammals, such as the woodchuck or the chipmunk, are either dormant or in hibernation, the lives of small mammals are never so clearly recorded as after a fresh snow. Everywhere in the woods, the thin dribble of white-footed mouse tracks stitch the trees together; gray squirrel tracks appear abruptly at the base of one tree, trace an erratic pattern through the woods, and then end at the base of another tree. The single-line track of the red fox makes easy curves along the field edges, and rabbit tracks meander from one brushy cover to the next.

You would never assume from the records of comings and goings written in the snow that mammal life is not running at full throttle during winter. And, in actual fact, with a few exceptions, during good weather mammal life in the woods and fields carries on with only a moderate change in routine. There are periods—sometimes extended—when skunks, raccoons, foxes, and squirrels will remain secluded in their shelters waiting out a severe storm. But after the weather breaks, and particularly later in the winter, they will be abroad. The common belief that mammals hibernate throughout the winter is for the most part myth. In fact, in the northeast there are only four species that hibernate in the true sense of the word, the woodchuck, the meadow jumping mouse, the woodland jumping mouse, and the little brown bat. Technically, hibernation is a deep, death-like sleep, during which the heart beat slows dramatically, the body temperature drops, and respiration is slowed to a few sporadic breaths. The most famous hibernator of all, the black bear, merely goes into a sort of prolonged sleep for the season.

Nevertheless, for many species hibernation is one more method of coping with the test of winter, and it is a practice that reptiles and amphibians resort to as a matter of course. In some ways, since they are cold-blooded, they have no choice. With the coming of cold weather, frogs, salamanders, turtles, and snakes bury themselves in pond bottoms, stream banks, and beneath rocks and logs, where they are safe from penetrating frosts. Some species of snakes, particularly the venomous copperheads and timber rattlers, seek out rocky dens deep in south-facing slopes, sometimes hibernating together in a huge, tangled ball.

By January, hibernation, coupled with migration and the demise of the insect populations, will have stilled the woods and fields into an apparently lifeless landscape. The woods are barren walls of gray-brown, broad in the fields, a few errant flocks of winter finches may flutter past, beating against the wind, and occasionally, you may catch sight of the flash of a resident chickadee or nuthatch. But generally, this is the season of nonmotion. Whereas in fall, spring, and summer, the woods and fields were alive with the darting forms of birds and insects, signs of life are now relegated to events that occurred in the past—the wandering tracks of some mammal, or the scattered weed husks left by a flock of passing sparrows. Overhead, the sky is a seamless gray fabric, and day after day the woods and fields stand in waiting silence. It is the bottom of the year, the season of the Hunger Moon of the American Indians.

But like the span of summer, the bitter period of midwinter can also be short-lived. No sooner does the year hit bottom than things begin to stir again, and ironically, some of the most hopeful signs appear among the class of animals that seem to be the most thoroughly devastated by winter—the insects.

Not all adult insects die in the winter; there are a number of species, such as the mourning cloak butterfly, that hibernate for the season, and there are a surprisingly large number of insects that remain active throughout the year. On warmer days after midwinter, look on the south side of trees with deeply creviced bark to see if you can spot any of the sluggish, but handsome insects known as soldier beetles. If there is snow cover on the ground, at the base of the same tree you may notice what appears to be a sprinkling of black pepper. Look more closely and you will see that the individual specks periodically leap into the air. These are the tiny springtails, one of the most primitive insects on earth. A walk along an open stream anytime from midwinter on will inevitably turn up a few water-dwelling stoneflies. Watch for them crawling sluggishly across the snow, or look for them on tree trunks and mossy rocks by the stream's edge. February is the best time to watch for these insects, and if it is late enough in the month and the day is sunny and warm, you may even spot a mourning cloak butterfly winging through the trees.

February is one of the most interesting months of the year as far as natural events are concerned. The early part of the month may have all the characteristics of the bitter days of mid-January. But as the month progresses and the days grow longer, slowly, the great engine of the season begins to warm itself up. Birds such as the winter finches and the grosbeaks, which may have been present all winter, suddenly become more obvious. Early in the month in the deep woods, the nights may be loud with the mating calls of great-horned owls. By the middle of the month they will be raising their young, brooding on nests with snow clinging to their feathers. By day the mating songs of resident birds can be heard as chickadees begin to whistle the word "Phoebe" through the woods, tufted titmice begin to call "Peter, Peter" over and over again, and the cardinals begin to whistle like children calling a dog. What's more, the first hardy migrants may begin to show up before the month is out, and long lines of calling red-winged blackbirds and grackles will cross the evening sky.

From that point on, it is all downhill to spring. The sap begins to run, the buds begin to swell, the first hardy spears of skunk cabbage poke up through the moist soils in secluded swamps, and there will be moist days when the rich scent of exposed earth will float in the air for the first time since fall. At night, once more the huge sickle-shaped neck of the Lion will rise in the east, and the full 365-day cycle of the year will be completed.

The Winter Sky

Big Dipper

N

Little Dipper

North Star

Cassiopeia

Auriga

Canis Minor, The Dog

E

Orion

Taurus, The Bull

W

S

For Further Information: <u>Field Guide to the Stars and Planets,</u>
Donald H. Menzel, Houghton Mifflin.

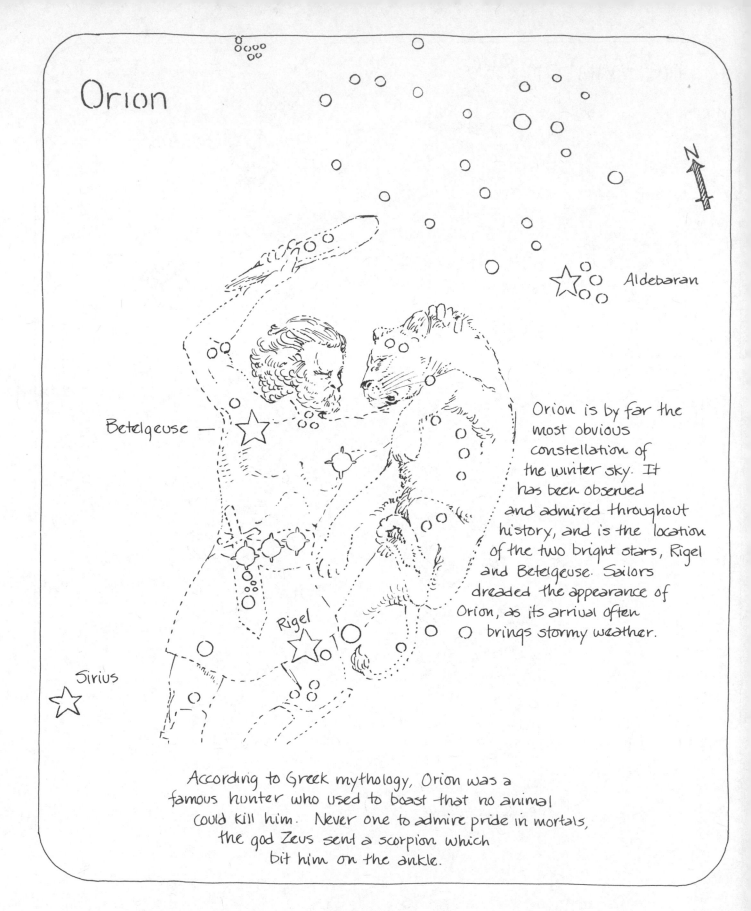

Orion

Aldebaran

Betelgeuse —

Orion is by far the most obvious constellation of the winter sky. It has been observed and admired throughout history, and is the location of the two bright stars, Rigel and Betelgeuse. Sailors dreaded the appearance of Orion, as its arrival often brings stormy weather.

Rigel

Sirius

According to Greek mythology, Orion was a famous hunter who used to boast that no animal could kill him. Never one to admire pride in mortals, the god Zeus sent a scorpion which bit him on the ankle.

For Further Information: <u>Find the Constellations</u>, H. A. Rey, Houghton Mifflin.

NATURAL BIRD FEEDERS

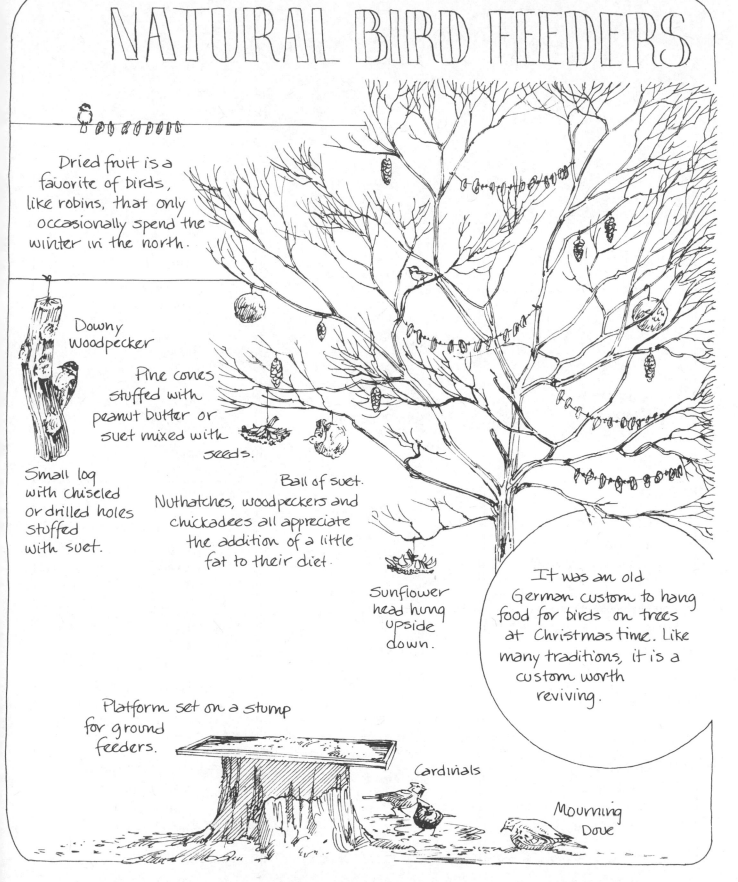

Dried fruit is a favorite of birds, like robins, that only occasionally spend the winter in the north.

Downy Woodpecker

Pine cones stuffed with peanut butter or suet mixed with seeds.

Small log with chiseled or drilled holes stuffed with suet.

Ball of suet. Nuthatches, woodpeckers and chickadees all appreciate the addition of a little fat to their diet.

Sunflower head hung upside down.

It was an old German custom to hang food for birds on trees at Christmas time. Like many traditions, it is a custom worth reviving.

Platform set on a stump for ground feeders.

Cardinals

Mourning Dove

For Further Information: <u>Watching Birds, An Introduction to Ornithology</u>, Roger F. Pasquier, Houghton Mifflin.

Food For Birds

BIRD	FEEDING PLACE	FOOD
Sparrows Mourning dove Junco	On or close to the ground.	Millet Cracked corn Small seed
Goldfinch Redpoll Pine siskin	Anywhere on or above ground.	Millet and hemp Thistle
Chickadee Nuthatch Tufted titmouse	Above ground, in raised or hanging feeders.	Sunflower seed, suet, peanut hearts, peanut butter, hemp, donuts
Woodpeckers: Downy Hairy	Hanging suet log or suet cage.	Suet Peanut butter Peanut hearts
Cardinal Cowbird Red-winged blackbird	On or close to ground.	Sunflower seeds Peanut hearts Hemp Small seed

For Further Information: *How to Attract, House and Feed Birds*, Walter E. Schultz, Collier Macmillan.

SPRINGTIME in WINTER

Many common birds begin to sing in late February, as soon as the days grow longer. Hearing their songs is one of the most heartening sounds in nature, a sure sign that winter is coming to an end. Weather has nothing to do with it. The birds respond to the change in light.

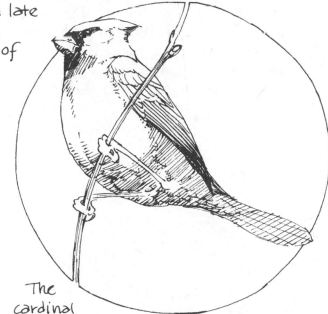

The cardinal song sounds like a person calling a dog.

Chickadees whistle the word "Fee-bee."

Tufted titmice sing the word "Peter, Peter" again and again.

Song Sparrow

Song: 3 drawn-out, sharp whistles followed by a series of short chirps.

"Ok-a-ree" or "O-conga-ree" is one of the most common sounds in the late winter landscape – the call of the red-winged blackbird.

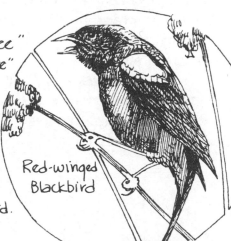

Red-winged Blackbird

For Further Information: How to Know the Birds, Roger Tory Peterson, New American Library.

HOW MAMMALS SURVIVE WINTER

There are only three mammals in the East that hibernate in the true sense of the word: the woodchuck, the little brown bat and the jumping mouse. Most other mammals are partly active during winter.

The beaver lodge is an elaborate construction containing various entrances and feeding and sleeping platforms.

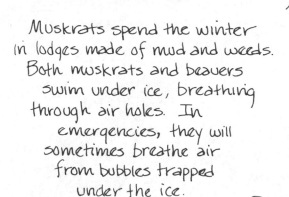

Muskrats spend the winter in lodges made of mud and weeds. Both muskrats and beavers swim under ice, breathing through air holes. In emergencies, they will sometimes breathe air from bubbles trapped under the ice.

Beavers anchor branches and saplings into the bottom of ponds and feed on them throughout the winter.

For Further Information: _Mammals of Wisconsin_, Hartley A. Jackson, University of Wisconsin Press.

There are days in winter when the entire landscape seems lifeless. Mammals stay hidden in dens and shelters, sometimes for days on end. Raccoons, flying squirrels, skunks, mice and other mammals will reappear on the first clear days after a stretch of bad weather. Watch for their tracks lacing the woodlands.

Most bats migrate southward a short distance. They are the only New England mammal to do so. The little brown bat is the only bat that hibernates.

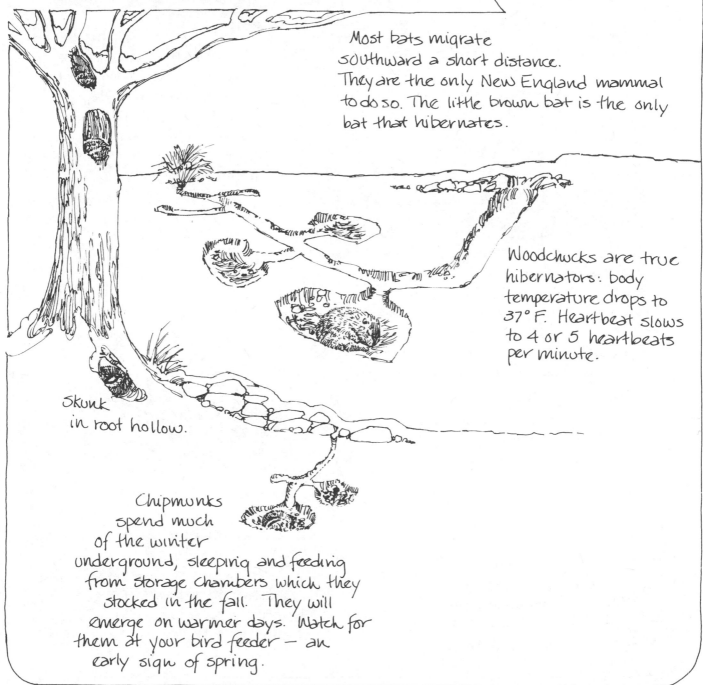

Woodchucks are true hibernators: body temperature drops to 37° F. Heartbeat slows to 4 or 5 heartbeats per minute.

Skunk in root hollow.

Chipmunks spend much of the winter underground, sleeping and feeding from storage chambers which they stocked in the fall. They will emerge on warmer days. Watch for them at your bird feeder — an early sign of spring.

For Further Information: _A Field Guide to the Mammals_, W. H. Burt and R. P. Gossenheider, Houghton Mifflin.

The Red Fox in Winter

Red foxes are naturally curious, and unlike many other hunting mammals, can sometimes be seen in broad daylight. Look for their tracks or droppings, or sniff the air for the faint, skunk-like odor that is characteristic of foxes.

Red foxes make their dens in root hollows or old woodchuck burrows. They mate in mid-winter and the young are born in spring. The yipping of courting foxes on still winter nights is one of the eeriest sounds in nature.

The red fox hunts by stalking its prey of mice, rabbits and meadow voles. Only rarely does he run them down like a wolf, or wait in ambush like a cat. Winter is a hard season for the red fox. Food is often scarce, and the voles and shrews are safe in their tunnels beneath the snow.

Fox droppings are about 4" long, and may have fruit skins and seeds in them.

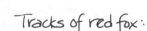

Tracks of red fox:

Paw prints run in a straight line. Dog tracks appear side by side.

For Further Information: <u>The Foxes</u>, Fred Johnson, National Wildlife Books from Ranger Rick. <u>World of the Red Fox</u>, Leonard Lee Rue III, J.B. Lippincott.

The White-Tailed Deer in Winter

During October, the white-tailed deer sheds its reddish, light-weight coat and grows a gray coat of coarse, hollow hair. The air spaces created by this winter coat help insulate against the cold.

Deer droppings.

Apple is one of the favorite foods of deer. Deer can sometimes be spotted in old orchards.

By December, the deer begin to group together to form herds, and usually retire to swamps or other protected areas to spend the winter.

Deer generally remain in a protected area throughout the season, trampling the deeper snow and sometimes eating many of the tender twigs. This area is known as a deer yard. In years of heavy snow, deer sometimes eat off all the forage in a deer yard and are unable to get at new supplies.

Deer tracks are narrow, about 2 to 3 inches long and have sharp points.

For Further Information: _Mammals of North America_, Victor H. Cahalene, Macmillan. _World of the White-Tailed Deer_, Leonard Lee Rue III, J. B. Lippincott.

Tracking meadow voles

The rarely seen meadow vole is actually one of the most common mammals in the Northeast, even more common than the gray squirrel. In late winter you can see their runways winding through the fields beneath the melting snow. Follow these tiny trails and you may find a nest, or a food storage area, or even a vole.

The meadow vole nest is made of woven grasses and rootlets. From the outside, it looks like a loose ball of grass. The inside is hollowed out and lined with soft, grass fiber.

Meadow voles are about 6 inches long, chestnut brown, and have tiny eyes and ears and blunt noses. In winter, the coat may be gray.

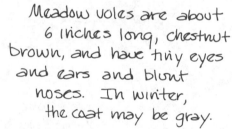

Meadow voles are active all winter long. They use runways on the ground level underneath the snow. In late winter, these tunnels collapse, showing the runway.

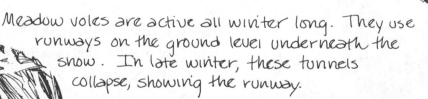

Along the runways you may find a cache, or food storage area. At the crossroads of the runways, you may find vole droppings.

For Further Information: <u>A Field Guide to Animal Tracks</u>, Olaus Murie, Houghton Mifflin.

A GUIDE TO SQUIRRELS

The squirrel family covers a wide variety of mammals, including woodchucks, marmots, prairie dogs and chipmunks, as well as the common tree squirrels. Winter is a good time to observe squirrels. Not only are they active during this season, they are invariably attracted to bird feeding stations.

Flying squirrels:
Feed at night. Stock your bird feeder with sunflower seed and shine a light on the feeder. At rest, they look like a small version of the red squirrel.

In areas where there are both red and gray squirrels, the reds will drive out the grays.

Red squirrels:
Have white ear tufts in winter and a red-brown coat. They are more common in northern areas in evergreen forests. Very noisy.

Gray squirrel:
Hardly needs an introduction. Watch for the bushy tail and the thick, winter coat.

Chipmunks come out to visit bird feeders on warm winter days. Watch for the back stripes and the upright tail.

For Further Information: <u>Wild Mammals of New England</u>, Alfred J. Godin, The Johns Hopkins University Press.

A GUIDE TO ANIMAL TRACKS

Wherever they go, whatever they do,
mammals leave signs. Winter is the
best time to track them, especially after light snow falls.

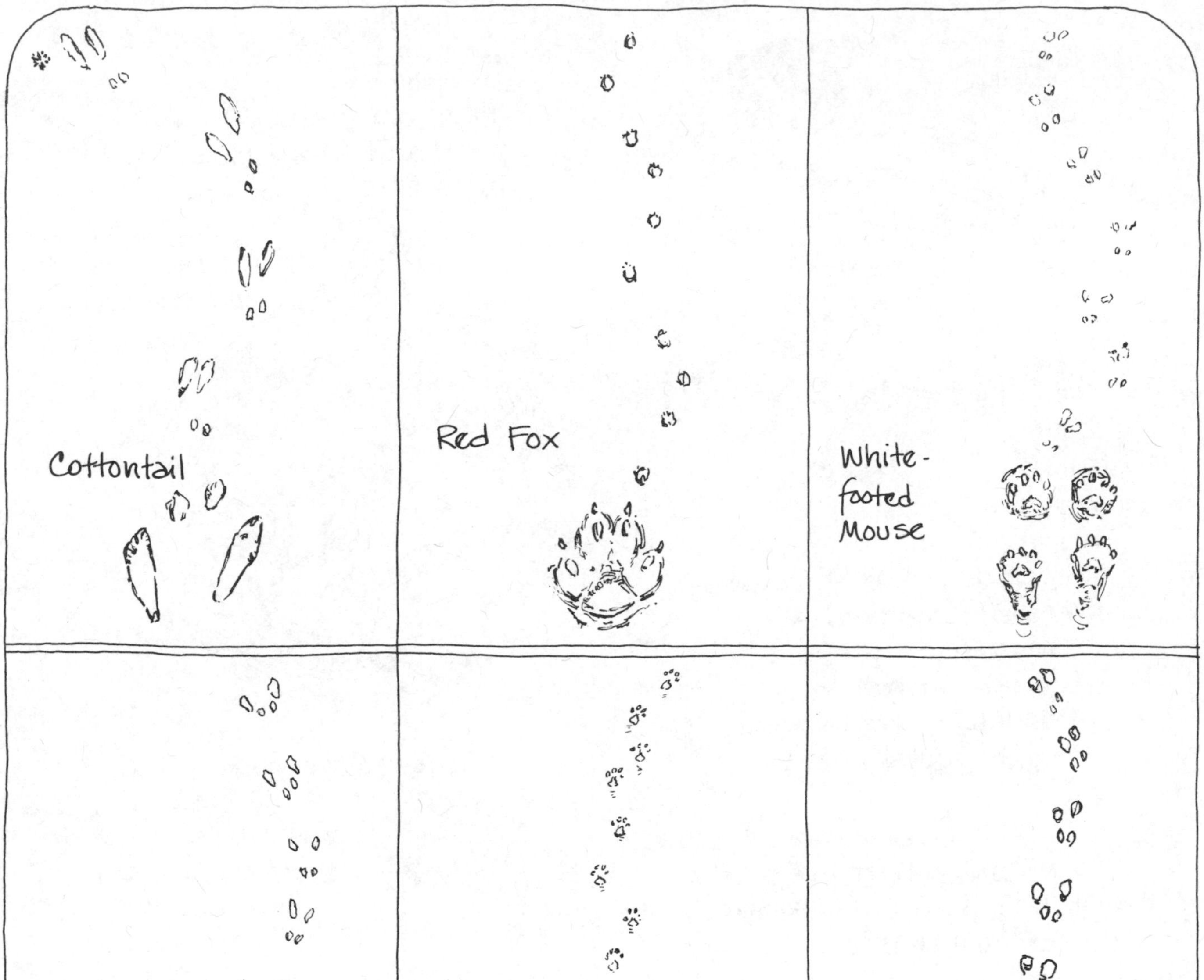

Cottontail

Red Fox

White-footed Mouse

Gray Squirrel

House Cat

Chipmunk

For Further Information: _A Field Guide to Animal Tracks_, Olaus Murie, Houghton Mifflin.

INSECTS IN WINTER

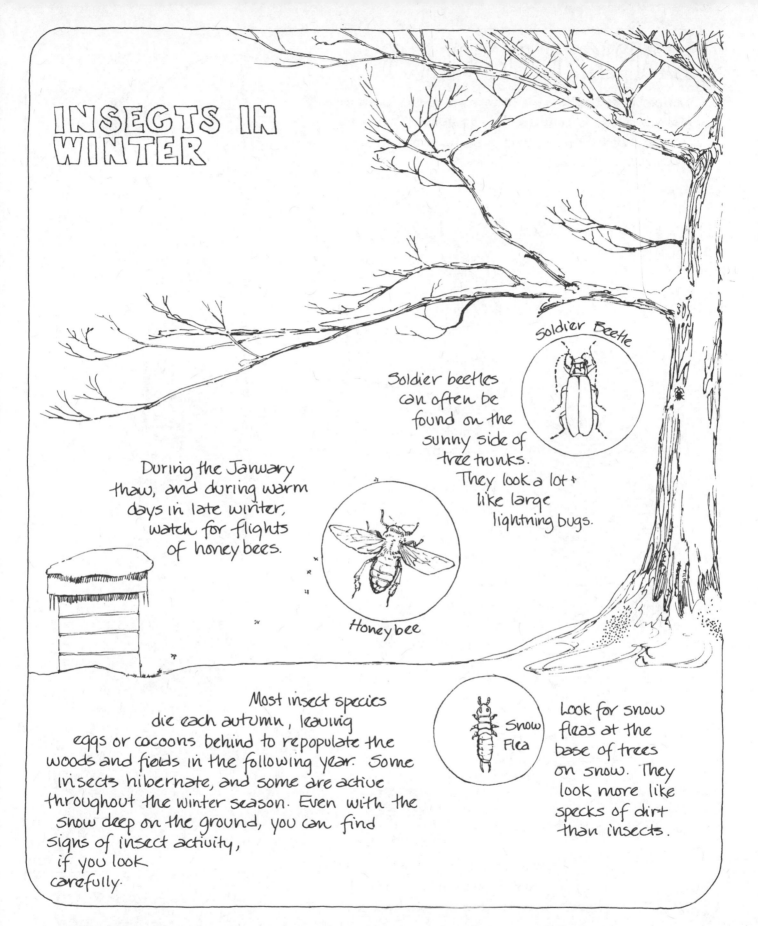

Soldier Beetle

Soldier beetles can often be found on the sunny side of tree trunks. They look a lot like large lightning bugs.

During the January thaw, and during warm days in late winter, watch for flights of honey bees.

Honeybee

Snow Flea

Look for snow fleas at the base of trees on snow. They look more like specks of dirt than insects.

Most insect species die each autumn, leaving eggs or cocoons behind to repopulate the woods and fields in the following year. Some insects hibernate, and some are active throughout the winter season. Even with the snow deep on the ground, you can find signs of insect activity, if you look carefully.

For Further Information: <u>A Guide to Nature in Winter</u>, Donald W. Stokes, Little, Brown and Company.

BARK BEETLES

Female bark beetles lay their eggs under bark in a slotted groove known as the egg tunnel. When the larvae hatch, they tunnel away from the groove, thus creating beautiful designs.

Spruce Bark Beetle:

In stumps of spruce trees. Prefers younger trees.

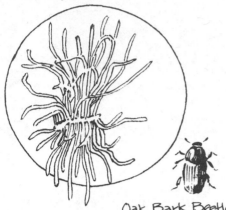

Oak Bark Beetle:

Watch for the confusing tangle of tunnels. Will live on other species of trees.

Ash Bark Beetle:

Tunnels are shorter than most bark beetles.

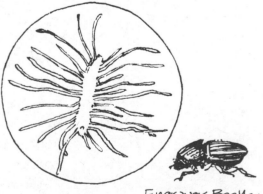

Engraver Beetle:

Common on fruit trees. Like most of the bark beetles, it is a favorite food of woodpeckers.

For Further Information: <u>Woodland Life</u>, G. Mandahl-Barth, Blanford Press.

STONEFLIES

Watch for stoneflies along any clean,
running brook that is free of ice.
Even during midwinter you can
find these unusual insects lingering
on stones or on nearby tree trunks
or bridges. Sometimes they can
be spotted crawling slowly across
the snow, and on warmer days they
will take off and fly lazily over the water.

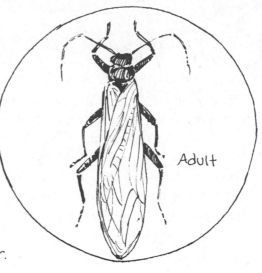

Adult

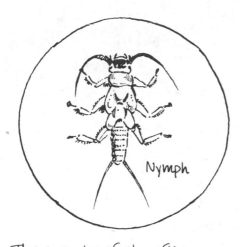

Nymph

The nymphs of stoneflies
live in water. In midwinter,
they emerge and molt into
the adult form. If you look carefully
on rocks along stream edges where
stoneflies appear, you may be able to find
the castoff skin of the nymph. Nymphs are
a favorite food of trout and
are often used as bait by
fishermen.

After they emerge from
water, the adult stoneflies
feed on algae growing
on trees and rocks. After
mating, the female lays her
eggs in the water. Partly
because of the cold, stoneflies appear to be slow-
moving insects. But if
you disturb them, they
will scuttle off across the snow,
with a rat-like gate.

For Further Information: <u>Field Book of Animals in Winter</u>, Ann H. Morgan, G.P. Putnam's Sons.

Snow Fleas

The next time you walk in the woods on a warm day when there is snow-cover, be sure to check the snow at the base of the trees. You may see a mass of black specks that look like sprinkled pepper. These specks are snow fleas, one of the most primitive of insects, and winter is the best season to study them. Look closely and you will see that periodically they spring like mechanical toys, thus their other common name— springtail.

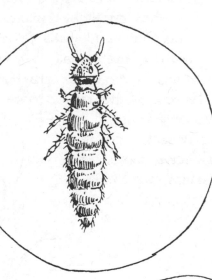

Snow fleas belong to the order of insects known as <u>Collembola</u>. Other species in the order are common around tidal pools, ponds and in garden soil.

Watch for snow fleas on the south side of trees. They appear to be more common in late winter.

Snow fleas jump by releasing two spring-like legs which they keep folded against their abdomen. When the legs are released, the insect springs upward.

For Further Information : <u>A Guide to Nature in Winter</u>, Donald Stokes, Little, Brown and Company.

winter trees

Winter is a good time to start learning to identify trees. Here, and on the next page, you will find some winter tree silhouettes. Once you have learned the shape, then you can begin to learn the buds and bark patterns. In spring and summer you can learn the leaves.

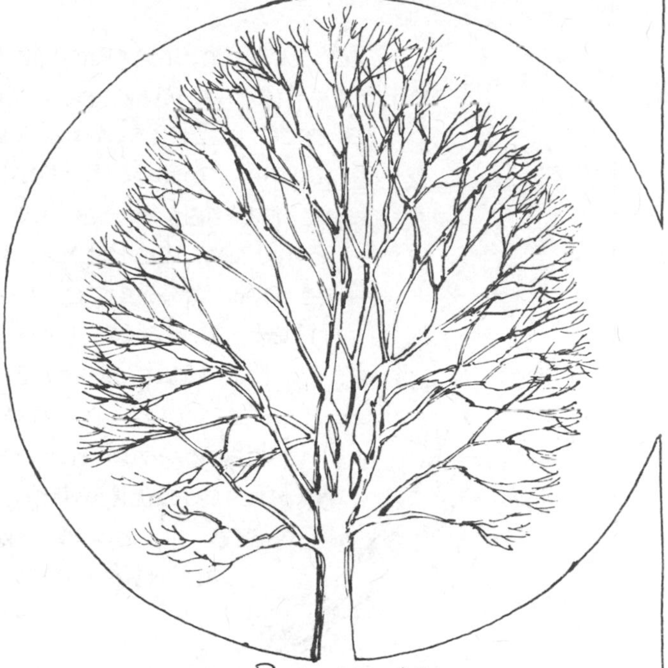

Red Maple

Shagbark Hickory: Look for the rough, peeling bark and scraggly shape.

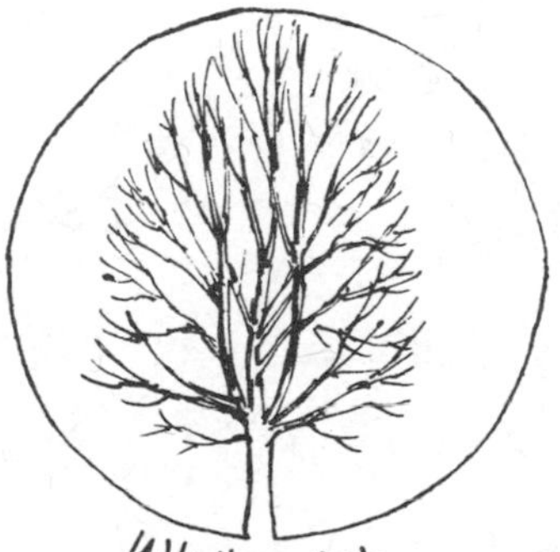

White Ash

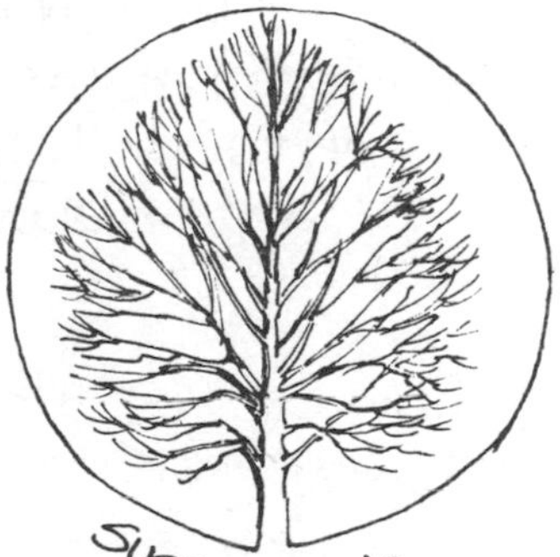

Sugar Maple

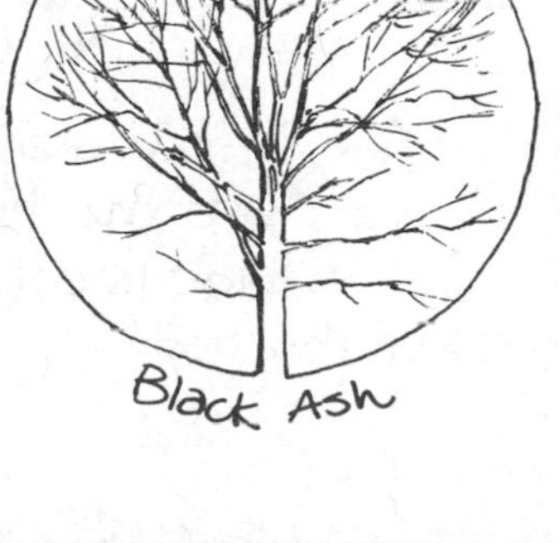

Black Ash

White Oak

For Further Information: <u>Native Trees of Canada</u>, R.C. Hosie, Canadian Forest Service.

Parts of a Bud

Everyone comments on the beauties of leaves, but very few notice the smaller beauties that make up the buds of a tree. It is only in spring when the buds begin to swell that they are noticed. Buds are formed in autumn after the leaves drop and can be studied throughout the winter. The bud of a tree is actually a small package that contains within it all the leaves for the next summer. The buds of each species of tree have a characteristic shape and design. On any given branch, there will be two types of buds, the lateral and the terminal.

Terminal Bud

Terminal buds are the large buds that appear at the very end of twigs. Lateral buds appear along the side.

Lateral Buds

Terminal Bud

Leaf scar

Lateral bud

Bud scales are the tough, outside coverings of the bud.

Growth rings are lines around twigs that show where last year's terminal bud was located.

For Further Information: <u>The Tree Identification Book</u>, George W.D. Symonds, William Morrow & Company.

Sugar Maple

Ash

Red Maple

TREES BY THEIR BUDS

Black Oak

Catkins of White Birch

White Oak

Catkins of Speckled Alder

Hickory

For Further Information: Winter Keys to Woody Plants of Maine, Campbell, Hyland & Campbell, University of Maine Press.

LEAF SCARS

When leaves fall in autumn, they leave a
scar on the twig they were attached to.
Within each leaf scar you will see tiny
dots, known as bundle scars, which are
the ends of the veins that carried nutrients
to the leaves. The leaf scars and bundle scars
make a pattern which is different for each
species of tree. Some of them take on
the appearance of faces. The leaf scar
is a part of the abscisson layer which
caused the leaf to fall.

Mockernut

Horse

Quaking Aspen

Greek Mask

Hobblebush

Sheep

Butternut

Camel

Bitternut Hickory

Hitler

For Further Information: A Tree Is Born, Sterling Nature Series.

BARK PATTERNS

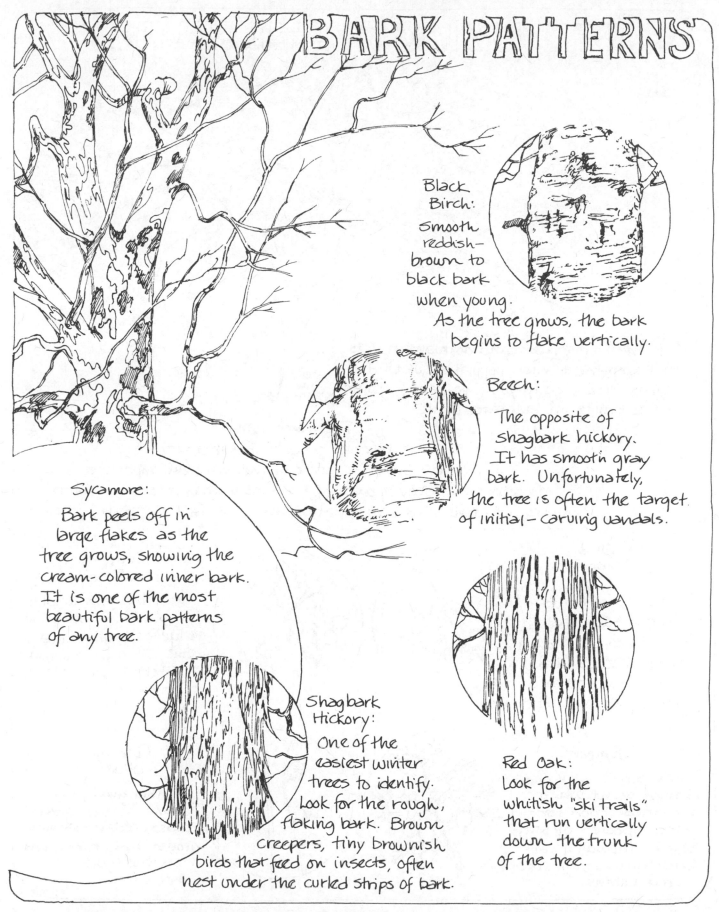

Black Birch:

Smooth reddish-brown to black bark when young. As the tree grows, the bark begins to flake vertically.

Beech:

The opposite of shagbark hickory. It has smooth gray bark. Unfortunately, the tree is often the target of initial-carving vandals.

Sycamore:

Bark peels off in large flakes as the tree grows, showing the cream-colored inner bark. It is one of the most beautiful bark patterns of any tree.

Shagbark Hickory:

One of the easiest winter trees to identify. Look for the rough, flaking bark. Brown creepers, tiny brownish birds that feed on insects, often nest under the curled strips of bark.

Red Oak:

Look for the whitish "ski trails" that run vertically down the trunk of the tree.

For Further Information: <u>A Field Guide to Trees and Shrubs</u>, George A. Petrides, Houghton Mifflin.

IDENTIFYING WINTER FRUITS

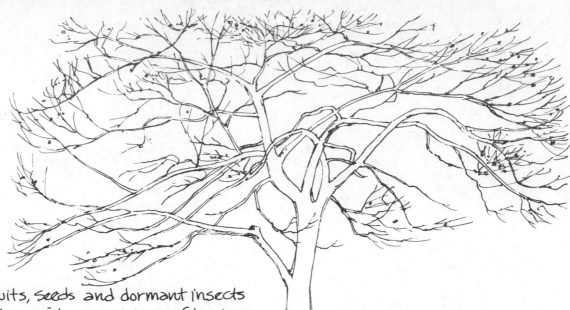

It is the fruits, seeds and dormant insects that keep the winter population of land birds alive. See if you can identify some of the fruits on a winter walk.

There are many different species of crab apples in New England. Some of them are an important food source. Many species of birds as well as possums, rabbits, skunks, raccoons and other native mammals feed on crab apples.

Wild Barberry:

Brilliant red fruits. Have a sour taste. Sometimes used in jellies. Mockingbirds, cedar waxwings and grouse feed on barberries.

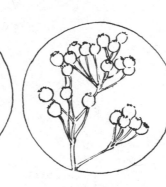

Multi-flora Rose:

One of the best wildlife food plants. A good hedge of multi-flora rose will often sustain a wintering population of robins.

Juniper:

Rich purple color and strong scent when crushed. Food for many species of song-birds, including cat-birds, finches, grosbeaks and robins.

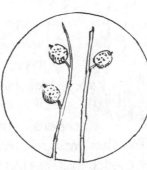

Russian Olive:

Another good food plant. Robins, gros-beaks, cedar waxwings, grouse and others feed on the fruit.

For Further Information: <u>The Tree Identification Book</u>, George W.D. Symonds, William Morrow & Company.

WILD TEAS for WINTER

Of all seasons, winter is the best for drinking tea. In general, a teaspoon of crushed plant material steeped in a cup of boiling water will produce a decent, warming brew.

Wintergreen is one of the most flavorful plants in the woods. Leaves can be used fresh or dried. Especially good with cream and a dash of honey.

Sassafras tea was one of the staples of the early pioneers. Boil the young roots until the water turns red.

Black birch twigs have the same taste as wintergreen. At right is the trunk of an older tree. Twigs have white dots, like cherry. Taste to identify.

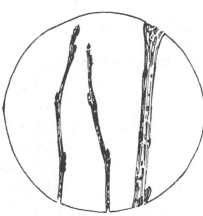

Hemlock tea made from the young tips of sprigs was a favorite of the lumberjacks of the north woods. The tips are also good when nibbled on a winter walk.

Spicebush has white dots on its twigs and a unique flavor. Can be dried and powdered and used as allspice.

NOTE: This is not the hemlock plant that killed the Greek philosopher Socrates. That was poison hemlock, an entirely unrelated plant.

For Further Information: <u>Field Guide to Edible Wild Plants</u>, Bradford Angier, Stackpole.

KNOW THE NEEDLES

Pine needles are, in fact, modified leaves. The shape helps the tree retain moisture throughout the winter.

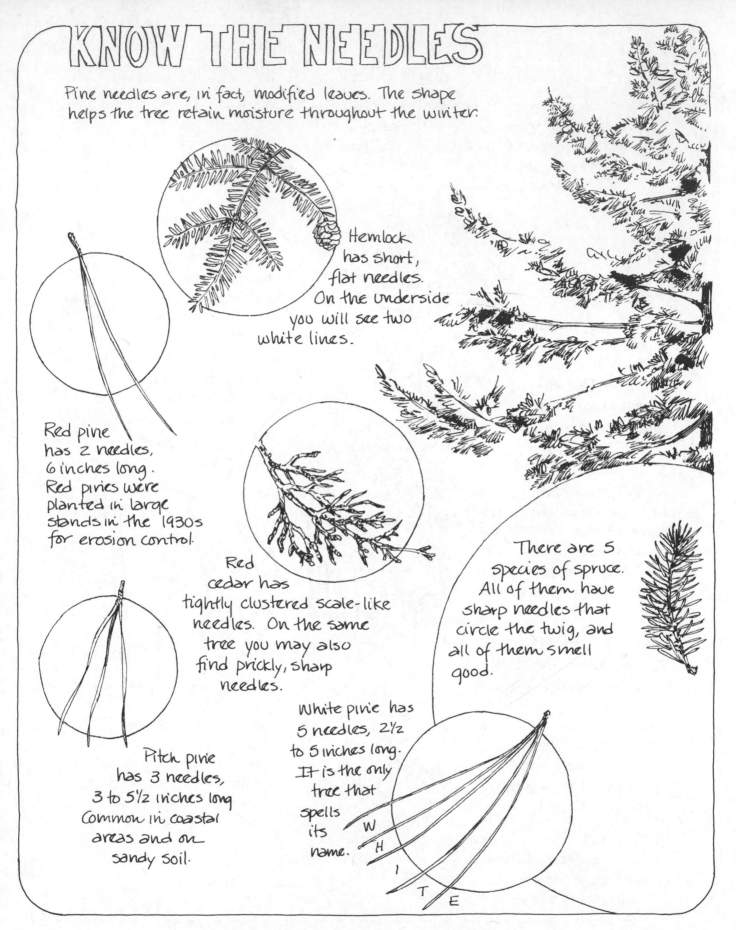

Hemlock has short, flat needles. On the underside you will see two white lines.

Red pine has 2 needles, 6 inches long. Red pines were planted in large stands in the 1930s for erosion control.

Red cedar has tightly clustered scale-like needles. On the same tree you may also find prickly, sharp needles.

There are 5 species of spruce. All of them have sharp needles that circle the twig, and all of them smell good.

Pitch pine has 3 needles, 3 to 5½ inches long. Common in coastal areas and on sandy soil.

White pine has 5 needles, 2½ to 5 inches long. It is the only tree that spells its name.

W
H
I
T
E

For Further Information: Trees of the United States and Canada, William H. Harlow, Dover.

Seeds above the snow

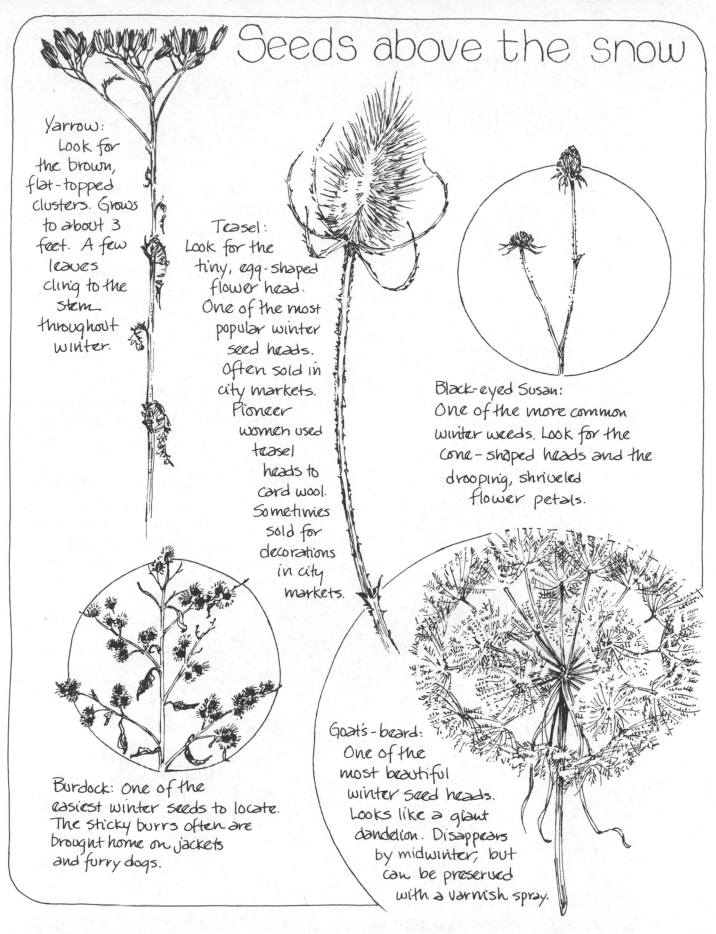

Yarrow: Look for the brown, flat-topped clusters. Grows to about 3 feet. A few leaves cling to the stem throughout winter.

Teasel: Look for the tiny, egg-shaped flower head. One of the most popular winter seed heads. Often sold in city markets. Pioneer women used teasel heads to card wool. Sometimes sold for decorations in city markets.

Black-eyed Susan: One of the more common winter weeds. Look for the cone-shaped heads and the drooping, shriveled flower petals.

Burdock: One of the easiest winter seeds to locate. The sticky burrs often are brought home on jackets and furry dogs.

Goat's-beard: One of the most beautiful winter seed heads. Looks like a giant dandelion. Disappears by midwinter, but can be preserved with a varnish spray.

For Further Information: <u>Weeds in Winter</u>, Lauren Brown, Houghton Mifflin.

backyard sanctuary
Feeding Shelter...

A simple shelter can be constructed by lashing a pole between two trees.

1. Lash stout saplings into a frame as shown. Any tree will do for frames but hardwoods will last longer.

Bird feeders provide a lot of food for smaller birds, but some of the larger ground feeding birds can be served better with a feeding shelter constructed away from the house at the edge of a woods or field.

2. Cut pine boughs and lay them around three sides of the frame. The open side of the lean-to should face south or east. Stock the feeder with cracked corn, whole dried ears of corn, and other seeds. Watch for pheasant, quail, or even grouse. And expect squirrels.

For Further Information: <u>How to Invite Wildlife Into Your Backyard</u>, David Alan Herzog, Great Lakes Living Press.

A WINTER GARDEN

You can enjoy the greens of spring throughout the winter. Fill a shallow box with soil. Plant with wheat berries, salad cress or parsley. When the plants are about two inches high, clip and use in salads and sandwiches. You can continue to plant throughout the season.

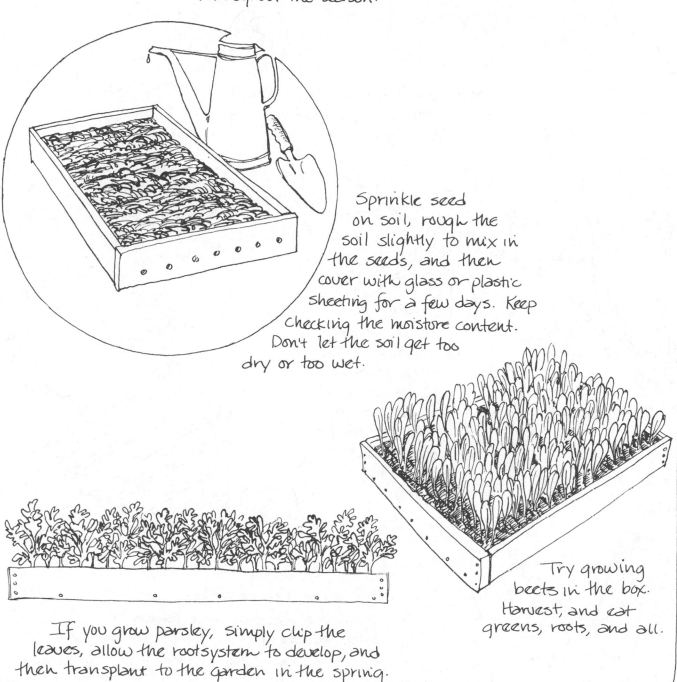

Sprinkle seed on soil, rough the soil slightly to mix in the seeds, and then cover with glass or plastic sheeting for a few days. Keep checking the moisture content. Don't let the soil get too dry or too wet.

Try growing beets in the box. Harvest, and eat greens, roots, and all.

If you grow parsley, simply clip the leaves, allow the root system to develop, and then transplant to the garden in the spring.

For Further Information: <u>Gardening Book: Indoors and Outdoors,</u>
A. Batterberry Walsh, Atheneum.

how to make snowshoes

If they were caught in a snowstorm, the Eastern Woodland Indians used to make snowshoes on the spot out of the trees around them. Here is one way to do it.

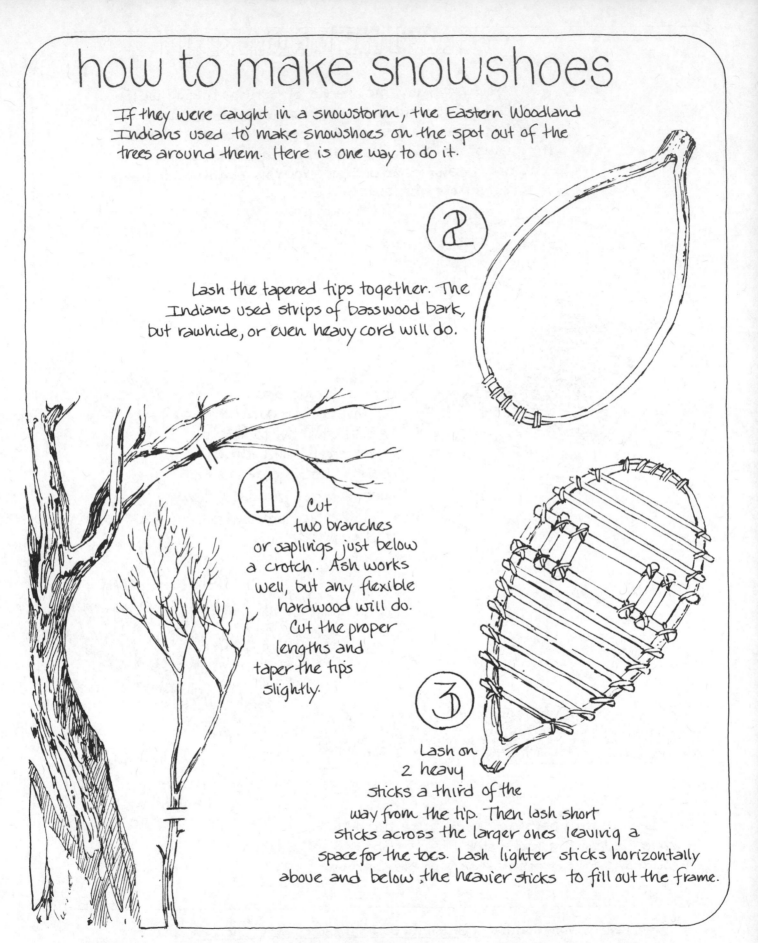

② Lash the tapered tips together. The Indians used strips of basswood bark, but rawhide, or even heavy cord will do.

① Cut two branches or saplings just below a crotch. Ash works well, but any flexible hardwood will do. Cut the proper lengths and taper the tips slightly.

③ Lash on 2 heavy sticks a third of the way from the tip. Then lash short sticks across the larger ones leaving a space for the toes. Lash lighter sticks horizontally above and below the heavier sticks to fill out the frame.

For Further Information: The Snowshoe Book, William Osgood and Leslie Hurley, Stephen Greene Press.

snowshoes...

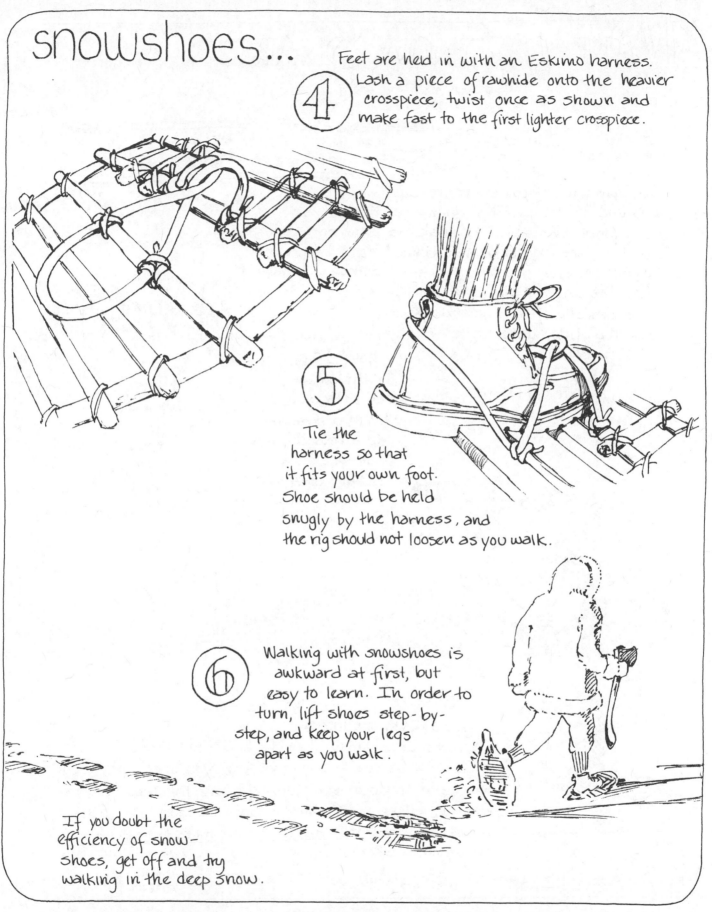

4 Feet are held in with an Eskimo harness. Lash a piece of rawhide onto the heavier crosspiece, twist once as shown and make fast to the first lighter crosspiece.

5 Tie the harness so that it fits your own foot. Shoe should be held snugly by the harness, and the rig should not loosen as you walk.

6 Walking with snowshoes is awkward at first, but easy to learn. In order to turn, lift shoes step-by-step, and keep your legs apart as you walk.

If you doubt the efficiency of snowshoes, get off and try walking in the deep snow.

For Further Information: <u>Nature Crafts</u>, Ellsworth Jaeger, Macmillan.

Make a Snow Snake

Throwing the snow snake was one of the favorite games of Iroquois Indians. The "snake" is a smooth stick about 5 feet long with an upcurved head. You can make one from a hickory or ash branch. Strip the smaller branches and bark, and smooth off with sandpaper so the stick slides easily.

Make a trail for the snow snake by dragging a log in a straight line across a field or lake. The Indians used to wet the trail and let it freeze overnight.

Throw the snake like a bowling ball, holding it at the end. You can play with as many individuals as you like. The Iroquois played in teams of six. Winners are the ones who can slide the snake the farthest. Good Iroquois players reportedly used to slide the snake more than half a mile on smooth lake surfaces.

For Further Information: Nature Crafts, Ellsworth Jaeger, Macmillan.

LOG-SIDED OWL HOUSE

You can make a house for a screech owl from a 16 to 18 inch length of log. The idea is to remove the center, cut a hole for the owl and then "rebuild" the log. Screech owls like old apple orchards or sparsely wooded areas. Place the house about 15 feet above the ground on a tree at the edge of the woods.

1 Split off 4 sides of a 16 to 18 inch log.

2 Saw off the ends of the core for the top and bottom of the house.

3 Cut a 3¼ inch entrance hole and replace the sides, top and bottom without the core.

3¼" Make the entrance hole 3¼ inches in diameter.

For Further Information: Easy Crafts, Ellsworth Jaeger, Macmillan.

Small Scale Maple Sugaring

Late February, when the days are sunny and the nights are still cold, is the time to watch the sugar maples. When little icicles appear at the ends of branches, it is time to collect sap.

Sap is collected by small tubes, or spiles, which are driven into the tree. You can buy or make your own spiles to fit into the drilled holes in the trunk. Be sure the spiles slant downward slightly to insure good drainage of the sap.

Almost anything will do for a container; buckets, tin cans or even jugs. Be sure to collect every day. And if you are using small containers, you will need to empty them every 2 or 3 hours on a good day. A good tree will turn out 20 or more quarts in 12 hours.

Sugar maples can be recognized by the branching trunk, rounded top and dark gray, flaking bark that curls on one edge in older trees. Twigs and buds are reddish-brown. Check your tree guides carefully to make sure you have the right tree.

For Further Information: <u>The Maple Sugar Book</u>, Scott and Helen Nearing, Schocken.

Boiling down indoors is possible, but it is a messy, long job. It will take about 5 hours to boil down 5 gallons of sap, and there will be a lot of steam, so be sure to open the windows or keep the fan over the stove running. When the sap "sheets" off a spoon, it has become syrup. For all the work, sugaring off is a worthwhile project. There is nothing like homemade maple syrup.

Boiling down the sap is a job that is best done outdoors in a flat, shallow container over an open wood fire.

Store the maple sap in a large container in a place where it will stay cool but not freeze. It takes about 40 quarts of sap to make one quart of syrup. When you have enough sap to make the amount of syrup you want, you can begin boiling down.

For Further Information: The Maple Sugar Book, Scott and Helen Nearing, Schocken.

BUILD A BLUEBIRD HOUSE

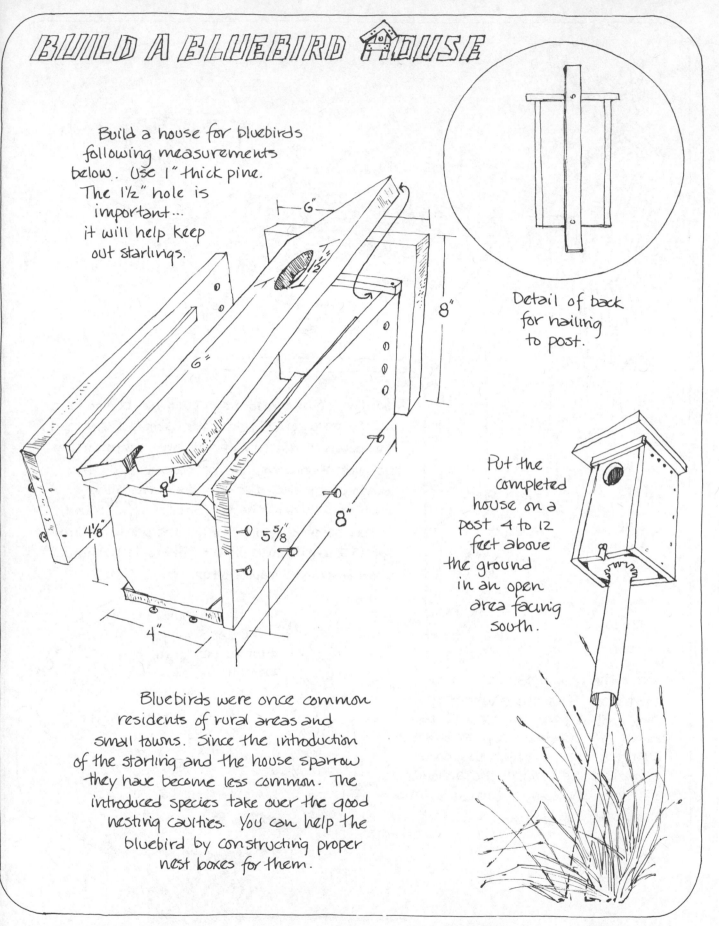

Build a house for bluebirds following measurements below. Use 1" thick pine. The 1½" hole is important... it will help keep out starlings.

6"

6"

8"

8"

4⅛"

5⅝"

4"

Detail of back for nailing to post.

Put the completed house on a post 4 to 12 feet above the ground in an open area facing south.

Bluebirds were once common residents of rural areas and small towns. Since the introduction of the starling and the house sparrow they have become less common. The introduced species take over the good nesting cavities. You can help the bluebird by constructing proper nest boxes for them.

For Further Information: How to Build Bird Houses and Feeders, Walter Schultz, Macmillan.

A CALENDAR OF NATURAL EVENTS

MONTH	1st week	2nd week	3rd week	4th week
DEC.			Wood turtles go into hibernation. December 21, Winter Solstice.	Mice feed on grass shoots and bark. Watch for tracks after first snow.
JAN.	January 6, Twelfth Night — traditionally animals are able to speak on this night.	Stoneflies emerge as adults. First heavy snows.	Mating season for raccoons. January thaw — watch for honeybee flights.	The Hunger Moon of the American Indian — the hardest time of the year. Mating season for mink.
FEB.	Redpoll flights arrive. Listen for fox yelps. February 2, Ground Hog Day.	Great horned owls nest. Skunks mate.	On the coast, snow buntings move northward.	Mating season for foxes. Red-winged blackbirds return.
MARCH	Geese and ducks move northward. Pussy willows appear.	Blackbirds return. Song sparrows and fox sparrows arrive.	First hardy flowers. March 21, first day of spring.	

BIBLIOGRAPHY

This bibliography represents a mix of both student-and adult-level books. If you are an adult beginning naturalist, don't be put off by the books for younger readers; there is a lot of accurate scientific information in children's nature books that is hard to find in other reference books. Similarly, if you are a child and you can read fairly well, don't be put off by the adult-level books. Most of the information is simple identification descriptions or stories about the life histories of plants or animals.

AMPHIBIANS AND REPTILES

CONANT, ROGER, *A Field Guide to Reptiles & Amphibians of Eastern and Central North America*. Boston: Houghton Mifflin, 1975.

DICKERSON, MARY C. *The Frog Book*. New York: Dover Publications, 1969.

HAWES, JUDY. *Spring Peepers*, Let's-Read-and-Find-Out-Science Book. New York: Thomas Y. Crowell Co., 1975. (Children's book)

————. *What I Like About Toads*, Let's-Read-and-Find-Out-Science Book. New York: Thomas Crowell Co., 1972. (Children's book)

LAZELL, JAMES D. *This Broken Archipelago*. New York: Quadrangle, 1976.

PARKER, H. W., and A. G. C. GRANDISON, BRITISH MUSEUM. *Snakes—A Natural History*. Ithaca, New York: Cornell University Press, 1977.

RUCKER, H. SMYTH. *Amphibians and Their Ways*. New York: Macmillan, 1962.

SCHMIDT, KARL P., and D. DWIGHT DAVIS. *Field Book of Snakes*. New York: Putnam, 1941.

WHITE, WILLIAM, JR. *A Frog Is Born*. New York: Sterling Publishing Co., 1972. (Children's book)

ZIM, HERBERT S. and HOBART M. SMITH. *Reptiles & Amphibians*. New York: Golden Press, 1953.

BACKYARD SANCTUARY

COOPER, ELIZABETH K. *Science in Your Own Backyard*. New York: Harcourt, Brace & World, 1958. (Children's book)

Gardening with Wildlife. Washington, D.C.: National Wildlife Federation, 1974.

HERZOG, DAVID A. *How to Invite Wildlife into Your Backyard*. Matleson, Ill.: Great Lakes Living Press, 1977.

Invite Wildlife to Your Backyard. Washington, D.C.: National Wildlife Federation. (Pamphlet available, 1412 16th St., NW, Washington, D.C. 20036)

MARGOLIN, MALCOLM, *The Earth Manual*. Boston: Houghton Mifflin, 1975.

BIRDS

KORTRIGHT, FRANCIS H. *The Ducks, Geese and Swans of North America*. New York: Stackpole Books, 1942.

PASQUIER, ROGER F. *Watching Birds, An Introduction to Ornithology*. Boston: Houghton Mifflin, 1977.

PETERSON, ROGER TORY. *A Field Guide to the Birds*. Boston: Houghton Mifflin, 1947.

———. *How to Know the Birds*. New York: New American Library, 1971.

ROBBINS, CHANDLER. *Birds of North America*. New York: Golden Press, 1966.

SHULTZ, WALTER E., *How to Attract, House and Feed Birds*. New York: Collier Macmillan, 1974.

SPARKS, JOHN, and TONY SOPER. *Owls: Their Natural and Unnatural History*. New York: Taplinger, 1970.

WELTY, NOEL CARL. *The Life of Birds*. New York: Alfred A. Knopf, 1968.

ZIM, HERBERT S. and IRA N. GABRIELSON, *Birds*. New York: Golden Press, 1949.

CRAFTS

ALDRICH, DOT. *Creating with Cattails, Cones and Pods*. Great Neck, N.Y.: Hearthside, 1971.

CHARNOFF, GOLDIE TAMB. *Pebbles and Pods. A Book of Nature Craft*. New York: Scholastic Book Services, 1973. (Children's book)

CHINERY, MICHAEL. *Enjoying Nature with Your Family*. New York: Crown Publishers, 1977.

FIAROTTA, PHILLIS. *Snips and Snails and Walnut Whales—Nature Crafts for Children*. New York: Workman Publishing Co., 1975.

FOSTER, LAURA LOUISE. *Keeping the Plants You Pick*. New York: Thomas Y. Crowell Co., 1970. (Children's book)

GRACE, IDA. *Nature's Colors: Dyes from Plants*. New York: Macmillan, 1974.

HUNT, BEN. *Complete How To Book of Indian Craft*. New York: Macmillan, 1973.

JAEGER, ELLSWORTH. *Easy Crafts*. New York: Macmillan, 1947.

———. *Nature Crafts*. New York: Macmillan, 1950.

KRAMER, JACK. *Natural Dyes: Plants and Processes*. New York: Charles Scribner's Sons, 1972.

LINSEY, LESLIE. *Wildcrafts*. Garden City, N.Y.: Doubleday, 1977.

MERAS, PHYLLIS. *Vacation Crafts*. Boston: Houghton Mifflin, 1978.

MUSSELMAN, VIRGINIA W. *Learning About Nature Through Crafts*. New York: Stackpole Books, 1969.

NEARING, SCOTT, and HELEN NEARING. *The Maple Sugar Book*. New York: Schocken, 1971.

OSGOOD, WILLIAM, and LESLIE HURLEY. *The Snowshoe Book*. Brattleboro, Vermont: Stephen Greene Press, 1975.

GARDENING

FENTON, D. X. *Gardening Naturally*. New York: Franklin Watts, 1973.

FINK, ED. *Look Mom, It's Growing*. Barrington, Ill. Countryside Books, 1976.

GESMER, ANNA, and ELISABETH GITTER. *The Complete Book of Flowerpot Ecology*. New York: Coward, McCann & Geohegan, 1975.

GRAHAM, ADA and FRED GRAHAM. *Dooryard Garden—Tim & Jennifer's Calendar from Planning to Harvesting*. Bristol, Fla. : Four Winds Press, 1974.

KELSEY, ALICE S., and GLORIA HUCKABY. *Growing Up Green—Parents and Children Gardening*. New York: Workman Publishing Co., 1975.

PHILBRICK, HELEN, and RICHARD B. GEGG. *Companion Plants and How To Use Them*. Greenwich, Conn.: Devin, Adair, 1963.

RODALE, ROBERT. *The Basic Book of Organic Gardening*. Emmaus, Penn.: Rodale Press, 1975.

WALSH, A. BATTERBERRY. *Gardening Book: Indoors and Outdoors*. Boston: Atheneum, 1976.

WIBURG, HUGH. *Backyard Vegetable Gardening*. Hicksville, N.Y.: Exposition Press, 1971.

GENERAL

BATES, MARSTON. *The Forest and the Sea*. New York: Random House, 1965.

BRAINARD, JOHN. *Working With Nature, A Practical Guide*. New York: Oxford University Press, 1973.

BROWN, VINSON. *How to Explore the Secret Worlds of Nature*. Boston: Little Brown, & Co., 1962.

HANLEY, WAYNE. *Natural History in America*. New York: Quadrangle, 1976.

HILLCOURT, WILLIAM. *The New Field Book of Nature Activities and Hobbies*. New York: G. P. Putnam's Sons, 1970.

KRUTCH, JOSEPH WOOD. *The Great Chain of Life*. Boston: Houghton Mifflin, 1957.

LEOPOLD, ALDO. *A Sand County Almanac*. New York: Oxford University Press, 1949.

PALMER, LAWRENCE E. *Fieldbook of Natural History*. New York: McGraw-Hill, 1977.

STOKES, DON. *A Guide to Nature in Winter*. Boston: Little, Brown & Co., 1976.

STORER, JOHN. *Web of Life*. Greenwich, Conn.: Devin, Adair, 1972.

TEALE, EDWIN W. *American Seasons*. New York: Dodd Mead, 1966.

TINBERGEN, NIKO. *Curious Naturalists*. New York: Doubleday, 1968.

WATTS, M.T. *Reading the Landscape*. New York: Macmillan, 1957.

WORTHLEY, JEAN RESSE. *The Complete Family Nature Guide*. New York: Doubleday, 1977.

INSECTS

BORROR, DONALD J., and RICHARD E. WHITE. *A Field Guide to the Insects*. Boston: Houghton Mifflin, 1974.

BUCHSBAUM, RALPH. *Animals without Backbones*. Chicago: University of Chicago Press, 1976.

DOERING, HAROLD. *A Bee Is Born*. New York: Sterling, 1962.

GRIFFEN, ELIZABETH. *A Dog's Book of Bugs*. Boston: Atheneum, 1967.

KLOTS, ALEXANDER B. *A Field Guide to the Butterflies*. Boston: Houghton Mifflin, 1951.

MANDAHL-BARTH, G. *Woodland Life*. London: Blanford Press, 1974.

MITCHELL, ROBERT, and HERBERT S. ZIM. *Butterflies and Moths*. New York: Golden Press, 1964.

MORGAN, ANN H. *Fieldbook of Animals in Winter*. New York: G. P. Putnam's Sons, 1939.

NEWMAN, L.H. *Man and Insects*. New York: Natural History Press, 1966.

SELSOM, MILLICENT E. *Questions and Answers about Ants*. New York: Scholastic Book Services, 1967.

SWAN, LESTER A., and CHARLES S. PAPP. *Common Insects of North America*. New York: Harper & Row, 1972.

ZIM, HERBERT S. *Insects*. New York: Golden Press, 1951.

INVERTEBRATES

BURCH, JOHN B. *How to Know the Eastern Land Snails*. Dubuque, Iowa: Wm. C. Brown Company, 1966.

MAMMALS

BURT, W. H., and R. P. GOSSENHEIDER. *A Field Guide to the Mammals*. Boston: Houghton Mifflin, 1976.

BROWN, VINSON. *How to Understand Animal Talk*. Boston: Little, Brown & Co., 1958.

CAHALENE, VICTOR H. *Mammals of North America*. New York: Macmillan, 1966.

JACKSON, HARTLEY A. *Mammals of Wisconsin*. Madison: University of Wisconsin Press, 1961.

JARRELL, RANDALL. *A Bat Is Born*. New York: Doubleday, 1978.

JOHNSON, FRED. *The Foxes*. Washington, D.C.: National Wildlife Books from Ranger Rick, 1973.

MATTHIESSEN, PETER. *Wildlife in America*. New York: Penguin, 1978.

MORRIS, DESMOND. *The Mammals*. New York: Harper & Row, 1965.

MURIE, OLAUS. *A Field Guide to Animal Tracks*. Boston: Houghton Mifflin, 1975.

ROTH, CHARLES E. *An Introduction to Massachusetts Mammals*. Lincoln, Mass.: Massachusetts Audubon Society, 1978.

———*The Quality of Mercy*. Lincoln, Mass.: Massachusetts Audubon Society, 1977.

RUE, LEONARD LEE, III. *World of the Red Fox.* New York: J. B. Lippincott, 1969.

———*World of the White Tailed Deer.* New York: J. B. Lippincott, 1962.

SELSOM, MILLICENT. *A First Look at Mammals.* New York: Walker & Co., 1973.

NONFLOWERING PLANTS

BLAND, JOHN. *Forests of Lilliput: The Realm of Mosses and Lichens.* Englewood Cliffs, N.J.: Prentice-Hall, 1971.

BRIGHTMAN, F.H., and B.E. NICHOLSON. *Oxford Book of Flowerless Plants.* New York: Oxford University Press, 1966.

COBB, BOUGHTON. *A Field Guide to the Ferns.* Boston: Houghton Mifflin, 1956.

CONKLIN, GLADYS. *Fairy Rings and Other Mushrooms.* New York: Holiday House, 1973. (Children's book)

FROMAN, ROBERT. *Mushrooms and Molds.* New York: Thomas Y. Crowell Co., 1972. (Children's book)

HUTCHINS, ROSS E. *Plants Without Leaves.* New York: Dodd, Mead, 1966.

MILLER, ORSON K., Jr. *Mushrooms of North America.* New York: E. P. Dutton & Co., 1977.

NOAILLES, CUILCHER E. *A Fern is Born.* New York: Sterling Nature Series, 1971. (Children's book)

SHUTTLESWORTH, FREDERICK S., HERBERT S. ZIM. *Non-Flowering Plants.* New York: Golden Press, 1967.

SMITH, ALEXANDER. *Mushroom Hunter's Field Guide.* New York: Scribner's, 1977.

WILEY, FARIDA. *Ferns of the Northeastern U.S.* New York: Dover Publications, 1973.

HERBACEOUS PLANTS

BROWN, LAUREN. *Weeds in Winter.* Boston: Houghton Mifflin, 1977.

DANA, MRS. WILLIAM STARR. *How to Know the Wild Flowers.* New York: Dover Publications, 1963.

DOWDEN, ANNE OPHELIA. *The Blossoms on the Bough, Wild Green Things in the City.* New York: Thomas Y. Crowell Co., 1975.

GENAMING, ELIZABETH. *Maple Harvest.* New York: Coward, McCann, & Geoghegan 1976. (Children's book)

HITCHCOCK, A.S., and PETER SMITH. *Manual of the Grasses of the U.S.* 2 vols. New York: Dover Publications, 1971.

HUXLEY, ANTHONY. *Garden Annuals and Bulbs.* New York: Macmillan, 1970.

JORDAN, HELENE J. *Seeds by Wind and Water.* New York: Thomas Y. Crowell Co., 1962. (Children's Book)

MARTIN, ALEXANDER C. *American Wildlife and Plants.* New York: Dover Publications, 1951.

———. *Weeds,* New York: Golden Guide, 1973.

MILNE, LOUIS and MARGERY MILNE. *Because of a Flower.* New York: Atheneum, 1975.

NEWCOMB, LAURENCE. *Newcomb's Wildflower Guide.* Boston: Little, Brown & Co., 1977. (Illustrated by Gordon Morrison).

PETERSON, MAUDE GRIDLEY. *How to Know Wild Fruits.* New York: Dover Publications, 1973.

PETERSON, ROGER TORY. *Field Guide to Wild Flowers*. Boston: Houghton Mifflin, 1974.

SILVERMAN, MAIDA. *A City Herbal*. New York: Alfred A. Knopf, 1977.

U.S. DEPT. OF AGRICULTURE. *Common Weeds of the United States*. New York: Dover Publications, 1970.

ZIM, HERBERT S., ALEXANDER C. MARTIN. *Flowers*. New York: Golden Press, 1950.

POND LIFE

BUCK, MARGARET WARING. *In Ponds and Streams*. New York: Abingdon Press, 1955. (Children's book)

BUSCH, PHYLLIS. *Puddles and Ponds*. New York: World, 1969. (Children's book)

HOFFMAN, MILITA. *A Trip to the Pond*. New York: Doubleday, 1966.

KLOTS, ELSIE B. *New Field Book of Fresh Water Life*. New York: G.P. Putnam's Sons, 1966.

MEYHEW, SHIRLEY W. *Seasons of a Vineyard Pond*. Vineyard Haven, Mass.: Felix Neck Press, 1975.

MORGAN, ANN H. *Field Book of Ponds and Streams*. New York: G. P. Putnam's Sons, 1930.

REID, GEORGE K. *Pond Life*. New York: Golden Press, 1967.

ROBINSON, CARMELITA. *Life in a Pond*. New York: Golden Press, 1967.

WATERS, J., and K. MIZUMURA. *Neighborhood Puddle*. New York: Frederick Warne & Co., 1971.

SOIL

EVANS, EVA KNOX. *The Dirt Bok*. Boston: Little, Brown & Co., 1969.

SCHALLER, FREDERICK. *Soil Animals*. Ann Arbor: University of Michigan Press, 1968.

SIMON, SEYMOUR. *A Handful of Soil*. New York: Hawthorn Books, 1970.

Soils and Men. U. S. Department of Agriculture, Yearbook of Agriculture, 1938.

STARS

MAYALL, NEWTON R. *The Sky Observer's Guide*. New York: Golden Guide, 1965.

MENZEL, DONALD H. *Field Guide to the Stars and Planets*. Boston: Houghton Mifflin, 1964.

OLCOTT, WILLIAM T. *Field Book of the Skies*. New York: G.P. Putnam's Sons, 1954.

REY, H.A. *Find the Constellations*. Boston: Houghton Mifflin, 1976.

————. *The Stars: A New Way to See Them*. Boston: Houghton Mifflin, 1976.

ZIM, HERBERT S., and ROBERT H. BAKER. *Stars*. New York: Golden Nature Guide, 1951.

TREES AND SHRUBS

BROCKMAN, ZIM and MERRILLEES BROCKMAN. *Trees of North America*. New York: Golden Press, 1968.

DOWDEN, ANNE OPHELIA. *The Blossom on the Bough*. New York: Thomas Y. Crowell Co., 1975.

EDWARDS, JOAN. *Caring for Trees on City Streets*. New York: Scribner's, 1975.

GALLOB, EDWARD. *City Leaves, City Trees*. New York: Scribner's, 1972.

GUILCHER, JEAN M., and R.H. NOAILLES. *A Tree is Born*. New York: Sterling Nature Series, 1960.

HARLOW, WILLIAM H. *Trees of the United States and Canada*. New York: Dover Publications, 1942.

HOSIE, R. C. *Native Trees of Canada*. Ottawa: Canadian Forestry Service, 1973.

PETRIDES, GEORGE A. *A Field Guide to Trees and Shrubs*. Boston: Houghton Mifflin, 1973.

PLATT, RUTHERFORD. *The Great American Forest*. Englewood Cliffs, N.J.: Prentice-Hall, 1965.

POPORNY, J. *Trees of Parks And Gardens*. London: Spring Books, 1967.

ROGERS, WALTER C. *Trees Flowers*. New York: Dover Publications, 1935.

SYMONDS, GEORGE W. D. *The Shrub Identification Book*. New York: M. Barrows & Co., 1963.

————*The Tree Identification Book*. New York: M. Barrows & Co., 1973.

WATTS, MAY THEILGAARD. *Master Tree Finder*. Berkeley, Calif.: Nature Study Guide, 1963.

TRACKS

ENNION, E.A.R., and N. TINBERGEN. *Tracks.*

London: Oxford University Press, 1968.

MURIE, OLAUS. *A Field Guide to Animal Tracks*. Boston: Houghton Mifflin, 1975.

WEATHER

CALDER, NIGEL. *The Weather Machine*. New York: The Viking Press, 1974.

LEE, ALBERT. *Weather Wisdom*. New York: Doubleday, 1976.

SLOANE, ERIC. *Eric Sloane's Weather Book*. New York: Hawthorn Books, 1977.

————. *Folklore of American Weather*. New York: Hawthorn Books, 1976.

THOMPSON, PHILIP D., and ROBERT O'BRIEN. *Weather*. New York: Time-Life Books, 1968.

WATTS, ALAN. *Instant Weather Forecasting*. New York: Dodd Mead, 1975.

ZIM, HERBERT S., PAUL E. LEHR, and R. WILL BURNET. *Weather*. New York: Golden Press, 1957

WILD FOOD

ANGIER, BRADFORD. *Field Guide to Edible Wild Plants*. New York: Stackpole, 1974.

DENSMORE, FRANCES. *How Indians Use Wild Plants for Food, Medicine and Crafts*. New York: Dover, 1974.

GIBBONS, EUELL. *Stalking the Healthful Herbs*. New York: David McKay Co. 1970.

————. *Stalking the Wild Asparagus*. New York: David McKay Co., 1971.

HALL, ALAN. *The Wild Food Trailguide*. New York: Holt, Rinehart and Winston, 1976.

HARRIS, BEN CHARLES. *Eat the Weeds*. Barre, Mass.: Barre, 1969.

HATFIELD, AUDREY WYNNE. *How to Enjoy Your Weeds*. New York: Collier Books, 1971.

KNUTSEN, KARL. *Wild Plants You Can Eat*. New York: Doubleday, 1975.

PETERSON, LEE. *A Field Guide to Edible Wild Plants*. Boston: Houghton Mifflin, 1978.

FOR FURTHER READING

In addition to the quarterly magazine, *The Curious Naturalist*, the Hatheway Environmental Education Institute of the Massachusetts Audubon Society offers a full list of brochures, pamphlets, charts, and similar material for both students and teachers. You also can order back issues of the original *Curious Naturalist* magazine which is mentioned in the introduction. The following is a list of available material:

PLANTS

Clues for Conifer Detectives. A simple key to 13 common species of conifers of central New England.

Trees—An Aid to Identification. A pictorial guide to some factors that help beginners identify trees.

How to Be a Twig Detective. Side 1 presents basic twig terminology. Side 2 is a simple key to some common twigs developed by May T. Watts of the Morton Arboretum.

Leaves. An enlargement of an end paper from *Field Guide to Wildflowers* by Peterson & McKenny. Provides pictorial leaf glossary needed to use basic plant keys.

Flowers. An enlargement of an end paper from *Field Guide to Wildflowers* by Peterson & McKenny. Illustrates the different types of flowers and their parts. Provides pictorial glossary needed to use basic flower keys.

The Plant Kingdom. An outline drawing of the plant kingdom family tree with drawing of representative species in each major branch.

Stages of a Gilled Mushroom. Chart showing four stages in the gilled mushroom plus sketches of several other forms of fungus. Includes sketch of poisonous Amanita.

How to Make a Terrarium. Side 1 shows step-by-step process of constructing a terrarium from glass and tape. Side 2 describes how to plant and stock a terrarium.

Make a Leaf Notebook this Summer. Description of Ink Pad, Crayon and Blueprint Techniques for making leaf prints for your collection.

Screen Planting by Donald Wyman. A 3-page listing of hardy plants organized according to soil preferences with brief introduction by Dr. Wyman.

Galls. 14 common galls—their appearance, location, cause, time of year found; also includes activities with galls.

ANIMALS

How Animals Breathe. Close-up photos and drawings of breathing structures of a number of different creatures plus diagrams of the way oxygen is exchanged in different breathing structures.

Some Information on How Animals Spend the Winter. Summarizes the problems that winter presents to animals and the responses different animals have made to the problems.

A Beginner's Alphabet of Winter Tracks and Signs. Side 1 chart with animal sketch, track, scat and other useful signs. Side 2 is a Basic Grammar of Track Language with sketches of stories told in track and sign.

Skullduggery. Has drawings of the skulls of different mammal types with information about the tooth adaptations to feeding habits.

The Animal Kingdom. A pictorial family tree of the animal kingdom.

The Parts of a Bird. An outline drawing of a Whitethroated Sparrow with boxes and lines pointing to the major body parts. Helps beginners learn names of body parts so they can use basic bird keys or describe an observation accurately.

Some Common Winter Birds in New England. A checklist with place to record observational data. Checklist is surrounded by drawings showing what to look for to be able to identify birds.

Flight Silhouettes. 26 birds are illustrated from *Field Guide to the Birds* by Roger Tory Peterson.

Roadside Silhouettes. 28 common birds are illustrated. From *Field Guide to the Birds* by Roger Tory Peterson.

Shore Silhouettes. 23 shore bird silhouettes are featured. From *Field Guide to the Birds* by Roger Tory Peterson.

Life in the Evening Sky. Silhouette of city and country flyers that are pelagic feeders: Martin, Swallows, Bats, Whippoorwill, Nighthawk and Chimney Swift.

Birds of Prey. Information differentiates hawks from owls. Drawings illustrate shapes of the four basic native hawk types. Shows also flight patterns.

Attracting Birds. A 4-page leaflet for beginners describing winter feeding and plantings to attract birds to the garden throughout the year.

Going to Seed—A Manual of Winter Feeding. A 4-page leaflet describing the best kind of feeds and placement of feeds for a host of common winter visitors.

Simple Feeders. Drawings of feeders made from common items. A chance for useful recycling.

Nest Boxes for Birds. A 4-page leaflet giving general information about attracting birds with nest boxes plus detailed plans for building a bluebird house. A chart listing dimensions and placement for bird houses is included.

Care of Young Wild Birds. A 4-page leaflet explaining the difficulties and procedures needed for rearing orphaned birds to a point where they can be released.

Temporary Care of Young Wild Mammals. A 2-page leaflet explaining the hazards of and procedures for caring for orphaned wild mammals until they can be released.

Amphibians and Reptiles. A sheet that summarizes the differences between amphibians and reptiles and gives the characteristics of each of the major groups of reptiles and amphibians.

Adult Snakes of Massachusetts A simple key to 13 species—11 harmless and 2 poisonous.

Adult Amphibians of Massachusetts. A simple key to 18 species—9 salamanders, 2 toads, 7 frogs.

Some Frogs and Toads of the Northeast. A chart listing egg appearance, egg location, number of eggs and color, breeding time, hatching time, length and color of tadpoles, and time tadpoles mature for nine species. Sketch illustrates frog metamorphosis.

Massachusetts Land and Freshwater Turtles. A simple key to 10 species, carefully illustrated.

Care of Amphibians and Reptiles. A 2-page sheet with advice on how to hold these creatures captive for short periods of time and how to properly release them.

Our Seashore Life. An outline drawing of seashore animals placed in the tidal zone where they most commonly occur. A list of the animals with a number is given in the lower corner. User matches number to drawing.

Ten Common Insect Orders. Chart states order, metamorphosis characteristics, mouthpart type, field marks, and examples. Border drawings illustrate complete and gradual metamorphosis.

The Monarch from Caterpillar to Butterfly. Side 1, a photo series illustrating monarch metamorphosis. Side 2 has articles on monarchs and milkweed and how to band monarchs to study migration.

Some Pond Creatures and Their Sizes. Outline drawings of 14 water creatures commonly found in ponds. A line the actual size of the creature is opposite each enlarged or reduced drawing. Useful on pond field trips.

How to Establish an Aquarium. Side 1 outlines procedure of setting up an aquarium. Side 2 suggests animals to put in aquarium and some clues to their care. Also gives directions for raising food for aquarium dwellers.

PHYSICAL ENVIRONMENT

Earth's Building Blocks. A chart showing basic atoms and how they are organized into living and non-living patterns of organization. An up-to-date view of the old three kingdoms concept.

The Rock Cycle. A chart of the basic rock cycle with brief instructions on how to relate it to water as a rock thus allowing children to see the rock cycle in a time reference they can understand.

Geologic Time Chart. A chart showing characteristic animals of the major geological periods plus mountain uprisings on 5 continents and major glacial periods.

10 Basic Clouds. A pictorial chart of the clouds with descriptions of their height and some indications of their meaning in weather forecasting.

The Water Cycle—A. A photo montage with the water cycle overprinted.

The Water Cycle—B. Side 1 as above. Side 2 contains Some Water Questions. This is seven photos illustrating some water problems with some key questions as captions.

The Water Cycle–C. Side 1 shows a drawing of the water cycle that emphasizes what happens underground. Side 2 shows the nature and importance of natural flood plains.

Wind Force Scale. A pictorial chart illustrating the classical Beaufort wind scale.

Salt Marshes—Food for the Sea. A diagram of the food chains in the salt marsh and sea along with some basic facts on the value of salt marshes.

How Pollution Affects Animal Life in a Stream. A chart showing characteristic animal life in clean water, the point of addition of raw sewage, the zone of active decomposition, the zone of recovery and a new zone of clean water.

Endangered Species in North America, Hawaii, Puerto Rico, Mexico. A 16-page annotated listing of extinct and endangered species. Key facts about current status of each species is given. Compiled from the IUCN 1969 study.

Man vs. Gypsy Moth. A 4-page leaflet contains a brief history of the gypsy moth problem, an overview of its biology, discussion of the role of spraying in gypsy moth control, examination of alternatives and recommendations for rational control.

Aids for Environmental Education Compiled by Margaret McDaniel. A series of 4 mimeographed annotated listings of useful curriculum projects, films, filmstrips and other aids to environmental education. The 4 listings cover Grades K-3, 4-6, 7-9, 10-14. This series was developed for the U.S. Office of Education Environmental Studies Office.

Aids for Environmental Education - Update I Compiled by Margaret McDaniel. These are supplements to the AIDS described above. There are two annotated listings, 1 covering Grades K-6 and the other for Grades 7-14.

A Curriculum Overview for Developing Environmentally Literate Citizens. by Charles E. Roth. An 18-page mimeographed booklet that behaviorally describes an environmentally literate citizen, presents processes useful in developing same plus a list of 179 concepts in natural sciences, social sciences, and humanities that are reasonably basic to development of such literacy.

Some Questions Asked and Answered About Outdoor Classrooms. by Charles E. Roth. An 18-page mimeographed booklet that asks and answers many questions dealing with the practical development of outdoor classrooms in both new and old sites. A nuts and bolts approach.

Beyond the Classroom. (trial edition) A guide to the use of the urban environment as an instructional medium. Package includes a general guide to urban environmental education; 2 packets of activity cards—one for each of the grade levels K-3, 4-6, and a guide to the natural history of cities.

The Farm Book. by Charles E. Roth, R. Joseph Froehlich. Illustrations by Russell Buzzel. This 96-page book is about 25 percent text and the rest beautiful colored illustrations that show a wide variety of farm plants, animals and processes along with farm wildlife. A very useful book for the non-farmer.

Solar Bibliography. Compiled by J. Scott Tucker. An annotated listing of books, magazines, and various articles for a basic understanding of Solar Energy and its application.

Wind Energy Bibliography. Compiled by J. Scott Tucker. An annotated listing of basic books, magazines, and articles for a general understanding of Wind Energy and its uses.

Wildlife Survival Packet. A portfolio of materials with introductory sheet and index on different aspects of endangered species and wild animal care. For teacher or older student use.

Ecobuttons. Buttons symbolizing "The Choice Is Up To You" is printed in 3 colors. The "good" side is in color; the "bad" side in black and white. These were developed as a fund raiser for ecology-oriented youth groups. It is a solidly constructed long-lasting button 2" in diameter. We sell them to you for 10 cents per button in lots of 20 or more. You re-sell them for 50 cents or more with the proceeds going toward your local ecology project.

Christmas Tree For The Birds. A 4" x 8" Christmas postcard with design on one side and description of how to decorate your own such tree on the back; along with address.

NON-MASSACHUSETTS AUDUBON MATERIALS

National Audubon Nature Bulletins

73 informative guides developed by the National Audubon Society for all phases of a nature program. Excellent line drawings and photographs. These bulletins are comprehensive, authoritative yet easy to read and understand. The entire set of 73 bulletins makes a *ready reference* notebook 8½" x 11", 4–6 pages. Junior High—Adult. By mail we sell these only in complete sets or subsets.

Complete Set NB 1 of 73 Bulletins

Subset NB 2 Good Teaching Aids 13 bulletins

Subset NB 3 Bulletins on Animals and How They Live, 13 bulletins

Subset NB 4 Bulletins on Insects and Spiders, 8 bulletins

Subset NB 5 Bulletins on Plant Identification, 14 bulletins

Subset NB 6 Bulletins on Conservation 10 bulletins

Subset NB 7 Bulletins on Ecology 9 bulletins

Subset NB 8 Flannel Board Bulletins 6 bulletins

National Audubon Nature Charts

Audubon Bird Chart color, 27 species 26" x 40" vertical

Audubon Tree Chart color, 50 species 26" x 40" vertical

Audubon Wildflower Chart (2), color, 37 species 26" x 40" vertical

Audubon Mammal Chart, color, 30 species 26" x 40" horizontal

One Color Wall Charts: 14" x 20", 14 charts

Catkin-bearing Trees, 6 species

Leaves of Common Trees, 41 species. Simple

16 species. Compound

Evergreens, 29 species

Common Seed Travelers, 35 species

Bird Study, bills, tail and foot types

Bird Migration, illustrated map of 16 species

Audubon Bird Calendar Chart 68 species and space for recording 25 species

Forest Food Chains, 28 animals and 10 plant foods

Amphibians, lifecycles of 2 species plus other adults

Twigs of Common Trees, 62 species

Lichens, 50 species

Mosses, 32 species

Salt Water Food Chains, 42 creatures and interrelationships

National Audubon Mini-charts

All one-color poster titles in 7" x 11" format. Sold as a set of 15 or in Classroom Sets of 1 full size chart and 35 mini-charts of any one title

Ecosystems Notebook with overlays

National Audubon Bird Leaflets

Leaflets describing the haunts, habits, range and other facts about one bird. By mail we sell these only in sets of eight on birds with similar habitats.

Birds of the Field

Birds of the Garden

Birds of the Woods

For back issues of *The Curious Naturalist:*

Volume I, 1961–62

Migration

Leaf Fall and Color Change

Seeds

Animals in Winter

Feeding Birds in Winter

Weather for You

Territory in Animal Life

Snakes

The Seashore

Volume II, 1962–63

Secrets of the Soil

Insects

Hibernation

Snow Geology

New England's Longest Winters

Water Birds

Water and Wild Flowers

Amphibians

Where Land Meets Sea

Volume III, 1963–64

Water Comes in Many Forms

Water Insects

Upstream (Fish)

Pastures of the Sea (Plankton)

Trees

Some Birds of the Woods

The Forest Floor

The Forest Parade

Volume IV, 1964–65

Wildfire

Insect Enemies of the Forest

Wildlife in a Woodlot

Uses of the Forest

Stray Dogs in the City
Plants in Winter
Digging into History
Snow
Turtles, Frogs and Salamanders
Robins
Flying Squirrels

Volume XIII, 1973–74
Climate—Plants—Animals
Deciduous Forests
Tropical Forests
Coniferous Forests
Deserts
Looking Back at Biomes
Mountains
Water Environments

Volume XIV, 1974–75
Food Energy
On the Move
Slowing Down

Fossils, Fuels and The Future
Solar Energy
Energy from the Earth
Energy from "Waste"
Balancing Choices
Energy of Nature

Volume XV, 1975–76
Lost Habitats
Hunters and the Hunted
Geography and Survival
Special Needs for Survival
The Alien Invasion
Wildlife and Man's Chemicals
Over-Collecting Wildlife?
Wildlife and Agriculture
The Ecology of Extinction

To order any of the above, simply send a large self-addressed, stamped envelope for a price list to: Massachusetts Audubon Society, Lincoln, Massachusetts 01773.

If you would like more of the type of material in this book, for $4.00 you can have it, each season, by subscribing to *The Curious Naturalist*. Below is a subscription blank.

Massachusetts Audubon Society

Lincoln, Massachusetts 01773

Name _____

Address _____

City _____ State _____ Zip _____

Enclosed: $_____

$4.00 ($5.50 Foreign)   Bulk subscriptions available.

Individual copies $1.25